ADORNO: THE STARS DOWN TO EARTH

The essays collected here offer an analysis of the irrational dimensions of modern culture which is both timely and disturbing in the 1990s. Adorno's ideas are relevant to the understanding of phenomena as apparently diverse as astrology and "New Age" cults, the power of neo-fascist propaganda and the re-emergence of anti-Semitism, and the psychological basis of popular culture.

The longest essay, "The Stars Down To Earth" offers a content analysis of the astrology column in a 1950s Los Angeles newspaper. Adorno argues that the column promotes psychological dependency and social conformism in much the same way as fascist propaganda. He maintains that the same principles operate in the mainstream products of "the culture industry." The three shorter papers illuminate different aspects of Adorno's argument: the relation of occultism to orthodox modern thought, the pervasiveness of anti-Semitism, and the "psycho-technic" rhetoric of fascist propaganda.

Stephen Crook's introduction critically reviews Adorno's argument and offers an assessment of its contemporary relevance.

Taken together, these essays offer an astringent antidote to any facile optimism about the democratic and pluralist character of postmodern popular culture. Adorno identifies an irrationalist dynamic which implicates the most enlightened and emancipated elements of contemporary culture. His unsettling arguments demand the attention of anyone interested in popular culture, critical theory, racism and authoritarian politics.

Stephen Crook is Senior Lecturer in Sociology at the University of Tasmania.

ADORNO: THE STARS DOWN TO EARTH

and other essays on the irrational in culture

Theodor W. Adorno

Edited with an Introduction by Stephen Crook

London and New York

First published 1994
by Routledge
11 New Fetter Lane, London EC4P 4EE

Simultaneously published in the USA and Canada
by Routledge
29 West 35th Street, New York, NY 10001

Typeset in Bembo by LaserScript, Mitcham, Surrey
Printed and bound in Great Britain by
TJ Press (Padstow) Ltd, Padstow, Cornwall

British Library Cataloguing in Publication Data
A catalogue record for this book is available from the British Library.

Library of Congress Cataloging in Publication Data
Adorno, Theodor W., 1903–1969.
[Selections. 1994]
The stars come down to Earth and other essays on the irrational in culture/
by Theodor Adorno; edited by Stephen Crook.
p.   cm.
Includes bibliographical references and index.
Contents: The stars down to Earth – Theses against occultism – Research
project on anti-semitism – Anti-semitism and fascist propaganda.
1. Culture. 2. Authoritarianism. 3. Astrology – Contoversial literature.
4. Occultism – Controversial literature.
I. Crook, Stephen, 1950–   . II. Title.
HM101.A442   1994
306–dc20   94-12151
CIP

ISBN 0–415–10567–6 (hbk)
ISBN 0–415–10568–4 (pbk)

CONTENTS

ACKNOWLEDGEMENTS

The editor and publisher would like to thank the following for permission to reproduce the essays in this volume: Chapter 1, "The Stars Down to Earth", *Telos* 19, Spring 1974, pp. 13–90; Chapter 2, "Theses Against Occultism," in Adorno's *Minima Moralia* (translated by F.N. Jephcott, London: Verso New Left Books, 1974); Chapter 3, "Research Project on Anti-Semitism," *Studies in Philosophy and Social Science*, Volume IX, pp. 124–43, reprinted by Kösel-Verlag, München, 1970; Chapter 4, "Anti-Semitism and Fascist Propaganda," in E. Simmel (ed.) *Anti-Semitism: A Social Disease* (Madison: International Universities Press, Inc., 1946).

The editor's thanks are due to Chris Rojek of Routledge for his encouragement of the project; to the Department of Sociology, University of Tasmania for material and intellectual support; to Rowena Stewart of that department for invaluable secretarial assistance; and to the Department of Sociology, University of Leicester for their hospitality during the completion of the manuscript.

INTRODUCTION: ADORNO AND AUTHORITARIAN IRRATIONALISM

THE CHALLENGE OF ADORNO

This volume brings together four texts written by Theodor Adorno between the late 1930s and the mid-1950s. The longest, "The Stars Down to Earth" is for the most part a content analysis of an astrology column in the *Los Angeles Times* which Adorno wrote in 1952–3 during a return visit to the United States from Germany. The shortest, "Theses Against Occultism," is on a related but more general theme and was written in 1947 as part of *Minima Moralia*. "Research Project on Anti-Semitism," a review of the dimensions and sources of modern anti-Semitism co-authored by Adorno, appeared in the journal of the Institute of Social Research in 1941.[1] The title of the final piece, "Anti-Semitism and Fascist Propaganda," explains its topic clearly enough. Published in 1946, the paper draws extensively on a much longer study which Adorno had written in 1943, but which was not published in his lifetime.[2]

These four diverse pieces by Adorno are underpinned by a (more-or-less) consistent and coherent account of the powerful tendencies towards authoritarianism and irrationalism operative in mid-twentieth century Western culture. That account is of much more than historical interest: Adorno's mid-century diagnosis is still, or even especially, relevant in the *fin de siècle*, postmodernizing, 1990s. Most obviously, there is no shortage of evidence that authoritarian politics, aggressive ethnic prejudice and extreme nationalism are still with us. The genocidal war in the former Yugoslavia and the resurgence of fascism in Italy and Germany are only the most prominent examples that euro-centric media place at the top of our agenda.

Coincidentally or otherwise, the period in which such irrational phenomena seem to have proliferated is also marked by a broader cultural anti-rationalism. It is a truism of debates about postmodernization that

1

the rationalistic "grand narratives" of enlightenment, progress and emancipation have lost their binding power in the advanced societies. Such societies evince a curious intertwining of dependence upon and hostility to science and technology. The anti-rationalisms of "New Age" cults, religious fundamentalism and deep ecology develop alongside and make use of the latest communications technologies and the latest findings in science. Adorno's diagnoses of the authoritarian complicities of astrology and occultism are directly relevant to these developments.

The remarks which follow do not urge a blanket endorsement of every element in Adorno's theoretical framework, each step in his methodological procedures, or every one of his substantive claims. There is much that is debatable, and a little that is frankly silly, in Adorno's work. But with all their infelicities, these essays throw down a challenge to students of contemporary culture to come to grips with the crucial, if unfashionable, problem of authoritarian irrationalism.[3] The main dimensions of that challenge can be mapped by three dogmatic propositions.

- Authoritarian irrationalism is an integral part of enlightened modernity, not to be thought away as historical relic, unintended consequence or marginal other.
- The affinity between modernity and authoritarian irrationalism must be sought in the psychodynamics of modernity, in the characterological bases and outcomes of processes of cultural, economic, political and social modernization.
- In their common manipulation of the dependency needs of typically late-modern personalities there is a direct continuity between authoritarian irrationalist propaganda and the everyday products of the "culture industry."

The three sections which follow explore each of these propositions in turn: while the four texts collected here are not (by Adorno's standards) difficult, their themes and contexts may not be familiar to contemporary readers. A fourth section offers a summary assessment of the contemporary relevance of Adorno's work.

AUTHORITARIAN IRRATIONALISM AS ANTI-SEMITISM: THE DARK SIDE OF ENLIGHTENED MODERNITY

Adorno's unsettling account of the modernity of anti-Semitism provides a useful point of entry into the more general analysis of authoritarian irrationalism.

2

For too many people anti–Semitism is nothing more than a pitiable aberration, a relapse into the Dark Ages; and while its presence is understandable in those nations of middle and Eastern Europe whose post-war status made the permanent achievement of democracy impossible, it is on the whole viewed as an element foreign to the spirit of modern society.[4]

This view, set out at the beginning of the "Research Project," is as prevalent in 1994 as it was in 1939–41. Indeed, there would be an added point: even for those who acknowledge the contemporary importance of ethnically–inflected prejudices and communal conflicts, anti–Semitism might seem a marginal issue. Afro–Americans, Australian and British Asians, French North Africans and the Turkish communities in Germany can be argued to be far more significant targets for racist politics than Jews. But, although twentieth-century anti–Semitism can appear definitionally linked to the time and place of the Nazi persecutions and eventual Holocaust, it does not go away.

Two German skinheads had, together with a Polish-born pub landlord, attacked and killed Karl-Hans Rohn . . . after beating him they poured alcohol over him and set him alight, declaring "Open Auschwitz up again, Jews must burn."[5]

It is not only in Germany that European anti–Semitism has re-emerged, of course. It is a potent force in the post-soviet societies of Russia and the East, while the far West is not immune.

Trevor Phillips, the [Runnymeade] Trust's chairman said: "this report shows that anti–Semitism is still alive and – literally – kicking in Britain today". Attacks include the desecration of a cemetery in Southampton last year with Neo-Nazi and anti–Semitic slogans, and the circulation of a letter accusing the Jews of the ritual murder of children. Rabbi Neuberger was one of many to receive a hoax greetings card for the Jewish festival of Chanukah last autumn showing a robin at a concentration camp, with the words "away in a chamber" and "God rest ye merry gentlemen."[6]

The ambiguous and persistent negative stereotype of the Jew, the "conceptual Jew" in Bauman's phrase,[7] portrays Jews not only as alien and inferior but sinister and powerful. It is strikingly easy for the criticism of established economic and political power to slip into complaints against the Jews: during the period of the Nazi rise to power the German Communist Party itself occasionally flirted with anti–Semitism, for example.[8] In our own time there are examples of members of disadvantaged minorities giving an anti-Semitic gloss to their grievances. The tension between African-American and Jewish-American communities in New York has hit the headlines more than once, while in Britain as elsewhere, radical Islamic groups flirt with anti-Semitism.[9]

> at night he is teaching young Muslims about their "enemies." The Jews, he says, are the most powerful force in Britain. "Who signed the GATT agreement for Britain? Leon Brittan, a Jew. Who signed for the Americans? Another Jew."[10]

The arguments of the "Research Project" considerably illuminate, even if they do not resolve, these difficult issues. Anti-Semitism is not an historical relic but "one of the dangers inherent in all more recent culture."[11] In a striking and provocative claim it is held that modern movements for emancipation and the modernizing process are both fundamentally implicated in anti-Semitism.

Emancipatory mass-movements from the first Crusade to the Wars of German Independence are analyzed and shown to display either a frankly anti-Semitic strain or some formal equivalence to anti-Semitism. For example, German universities in the post-Napoleonic period "combined anti-Semitism with the German ideology of freedom."[12] During the French Revolution itself, the aristocracy was marked as a "race" to be exterminated. Further, "there are a number of accusations against the aristocrats which correspond to the usual charges against the Jews – shirking work, parasitic character, viciousness, international connections, their claim to be chosen, etc."[13] The argument connects with Horkheimer's thesis[14] that bourgeois revolutions have always repressed egoistic and hedonistic demands, thereby producing aggression, terror and the perversion of hopes for "liberty, equality and fraternity." Modern anti-Semitism is the typical expression of that perversion.

On the question of "Enlightenment," the "Research Project" shows that anti-Semitic themes can be found in the work of the most ostensibly enlightened of modern writers, from Voltaire to Kant and Goethe. However, this line of inquiry does not bear much fruit in the "Research Project" itself where it is simply stated that despite their devotion to "humanity," enlightenment thinkers were "rooted . . . in the reality of their environment; their impulses, their intimate sympathies, and aversions derived therefrom."[15] No clear link is established between anti-Semitism and the logic of enlightenment.

This lacuna is largely made good in the later "Elements of Anti-Semitism" which Adorno wrote with Max Horkheimer. In addition to reflecting on the psychodynamics of Christian resentment of Judaism[16] and on what Jay[17] terms the "archaic roots" of anti-Semitism, Adorno and Horkheimer establish a series of links between enlightenment, conceptual thought, paranoid projection and anti-Semitism. The philosophical starting point is the observation that for epistemology after Kant "the subject creates the outside world himself from the traces which it leaves in his senses." It follows from the active role of the subject in projecting a conceptual framework onto sensory data to generate empirical knowledge that "reflection, the life of reason, takes place as conscious projection."[18] Anti-Semitism is not the antithesis of Enlightenment reason but a morbid version of it in which reflection does not set limits to projection. In such paranoid projections "the world becomes the weak or all-powerful total concept of all that is projected onto it."[19] Paranoia is a pathological possibility built-in to all conceptual thinking, the "dark side of cognition" and the typical symptom of the "half-educated."[20] Anti-Semitism is a form of paranoid projection which has long been at the heart of Western culture, and it can be expected to flourish as social conditions swell the ranks of the disgruntled "half-educated." This argument is central to the link which Adorno establishes between the "irrationalism" of fascist anti-Semitism and superficially harmless phenomena such as Astrology.

A more conventionally sociological theme developed in the "Research Project" which bears on the modernity of anti-Semitism is that of "The Jews in Society." In their historical identification with the role of "middle-man," with so-called "non-productive capital" and with "rational law" Jews embody those visible features of capitalist modernity which are found most objectionable in petty-bourgeois and utopian anti-capitalism.[21] Anti-Semitism is a nuance away from the "progressive" critique of capitalism, in a development of the well-known diagnosis of anti-Semitism as the "socialism of fools."

The account of Nazi anti-Semitism offered in the "Research Project" is curiously thin, superficial and unconvincing. It is argued, first, that "the replacement of the market by a planned economy of the state bureaucracy and the decline of the power of money capital makes possible the policy against the Jews in the Third Reich."[22] Second, it is asserted that Nazi anti-Semitism is aimed at foreign, rather than domestic, audiences. "While frank disgust for the anti-Semitism of the government is revealed among the German masses, the promises of anti-Semitism are swallowed where fascist governments have never been attempted."[23] These formulae are an echo of the tensions which surrounded the gradual and reluctant acknowledgement by the members

5

of the Institute of Social Research that Nazism was more than just another political shell for capitalism, and that anti-Semitism was more than just a diversionary tactic for Nazism.[24] Paradoxical as it may seem, Adorno's most important insights into fascism and anti-Semitism arise out of the study of non-fascist societies.

The arguments of the "Research Project" and related texts on anti-Semitism can be read in at least two ways which preserve their contemporary salience. One way is to accept that, for European culture, anti-Semitism is not just one ethnic prejudice among others but the very archetype of authoritarian irrationalism. The "conceptual Jew" is the defining and threatening other of, first, Christian Europe and, later, the Europe of national states and cultures. When other groups are singled out as the "enemy within" – aristocrats or Asians, communists or Catholics – they are endowed with a kind of honorary Jewishness. Alternatively, "anti-Semitism" can be read as a metonym for more general mechanisms of prejudice and collective scapegoating, for an authoritarian irrationalism which may take on different surface characteristics in different environments. Either way, Adorno's account of the modern prevalence of anti-Semitism/prejudice and its link with authoritarianism needs to be understood in relation to his model of the psychodynamics of modern culture.

FASCISM, ANTI-SEMITISM AND THE PSYCHODYNAMICS OF MODERNITY

During the 1940s the Institute of Social Research sponsored a series of investigations into anti-Semitism and authoritarianism in the United States. The best-known of these "Studies in Prejudice," *The Authoritarian Personality* [25] set the agenda for post-war social psychology with its claim that the characterological basis of anti-Semitism and fascism could be specified and be shown to be widely distributed. In the words of a contemporary reviewer

> anti-Semitism, far from being an isolated though unrespectable psychological phenomenon, is an integral component of a general "ethnocentric ideology" [which] . . . is revealed as the expression of a distinctive "authoritarian personality structure" whose unadmitted needs and defenses it serves.[26]

The concerns and themes of *The Authoritarian Personality* were not entirely new to Institute members. Earlier studies in Germany had developed a claim that the collapse of traditional family-based authority

6

would produce personality types susceptible to political-authoritarian manipulation.[27]

The account of authoritarianism and anti-Semitism developed by Adorno and other members of the Institute in the 1940s is heavily dependent upon Freudian theory. Freudianism was the vehicle through which the Institute moved away from the rigidities and superficialities of their earlier reductionist accounts of the phenomena. The dynamics of fascist regimes, fascist movements and fascist propaganda are conceptualized almost exclusively in psychoanalytic terms in Adorno's work. While this dependence presents a number of problems for a contemporary re-working of the analysis (considered below), it does not amount to a direct reduction of fascism to facts about individual psychology, as was charged by some critics of *The Authoritarian Personality*. Adorno's Freudianism is a dynamic theory in which the "self" is shaped and re-shaped in the interplay between what Freud termed the "psychic apparatus" and historically developing social and cultural conditions.

A useful point of entry into what can only be an oversimplification of a complex argument is provided by one of the best-known ideas from *The Authoritarian Personality*. High-scorers on the "F" scale (a measure of potential fascism) are marked by a bi-phasic ambivalence in relation to authority: they are submissive to those above them in a perceived hierarchy and bullying to those below. Elsewhere, Adorno identifies this pattern in a slogan of Hitler's, "responsibility towards above, authority towards below," and notes its sado-masochistic character.[28] The relationship which the fascist follower bears to the leader, a relationship which Adorno sees as definitive of fascism, is fundamentally masochistic. However, the leader permits, and sometimes requires, the follower to give vent to sadistic impulses.[29] A review of three issues associated with this relationship can structure this account of Adorno's theory of the psychodynamics of fascism. First, the question arises of how individuals come to be in a position where masochistic surrender to a fascist leader appears attractive. Second, the nature of the libidinal bond between leader and follower requires explanation. Third, these issues bear on the murderous aggression associated with fascism.

Adorno links the problem of susceptibility to fascist propaganda to the doctrine of the "end of the individual" which the Institute had begun to develop in the 1930s. The erosion of traditional family-based (paternal) authority undermines those patterns of individual development which produced that "mature" modern individual which is the subject of psychoanalysis. This development has a specific economic and social context. In a nice analogy Adorno and Horkheimer[30] liken the fate of the individual to that of the corner-shop which gives way to the economically more advanced supermarket. The individual is "the psychological corner shop" which emerged from feudal restraints as "a dynamic cell of economic activity." Freudian psychoanalysis "represented the internal 'small business' which grew up . . . as a complex dynamic system of the conscious and unconscious, the id, ego and super-ego." In late-modern society, however, the psychodynamically complex and autonomous individual is an anachronism. Individual decision and reflection give way in more and more spheres of life to corporatist policy-making and the repetitive formulae of mass-culture. For Adorno there is a fundamental symmetry between mass-culture and fascism, both of which feed-off and reproduce immature character structures with high, almost child-like, dependency needs.[31] Radio soap operas, newspaper astrology columns and fascist propaganda share the characteristic that they operate by at once meeting and manipulating the dependency needs of the pseudo-individual.[32]

In a discussion of Freud's "Group Psychology and the Analysis of the Ego" Adorno identifies the central principle as the "libidinal" character of the link between the individual and the mass,[33] and transposes this principle into his own account of fascism and fascist propaganda. Adorno frequently remarks that few fascist leaders present themselves as traditionally "patriarchal" authority-figures, a development he ascribes to the decline of the family: "as the father ceases to be the guarantor of the life of his family, so he ceases to represent psychologically a superior social agency".[34] He quotes with approval Erikson's characterization of Hitler as not a paternal Kaiser or President but "the Führer: a glorified elder brother, who replaces the father, taking over all his prerogatives without over-identifying with him."[35] This image of a fraternal leader is particularly well-suited to the libidinal attachment between leader and follower, an attachment which fuses elements of identification and narcissism. The leader's power and charisma function for the follower as a narcissistic projection of his[36] own ego-ideal, a projection with which he then identifies. However, the judicious leader must take care not to appear entirely awesome, entirely severed from the ordinary life of the follower. To paraphrase Adorno, the leader must remain enough like the follower to appeal to those elements of narcissism which remain attached to the follower's own ego. This is why, in Adorno's colourful phrase, "Hitler posed as a composite of King Kong and the suburban barber."[37] The fascist leader is the "great little man," embodying in enlarged form all the collective virtues of the little men who are his followers.

Two further points connect with this relationship, one of which will be taken up shortly and the other of which leads directly to the question of aggression. First, nobody who is now King Kong, now a suburban barber, should expect to be taken altogether seriously. It is a major theme in Adorno's analysis of fascist propaganda that it is in fact *not* taken altogether seriously by its audiences. As he writes, "Hitler was liked, not in spite of his cheap antics but just because of them, because of his false tones and his clowning."[38] These elements of parody, pastiche and simulation in fascism are critical to an understanding of its contemporary revivals. Second, and more immediately, there is consequential ambivalence in the figure of "big brother" who both stands in for and challenges the authority of the father: big brother can "sanction", in the name of authority, a collective violence which paternal authority itself would forbid.

Violent atrocities are much more than accidental "excesses" of fascism: for Adorno they are a manifestation of its basic psychodynamic principles in at least three important senses. First, aggression and destructiveness are at the core of the sado-masochistic ambivalence of fascism. Either more or less explicitly, depending upon context, fascist propaganda incites sadistic violence against the "enemy." German Nazis might explicitly demand that "Jewish blood must flow," while Martin Luther Thomas can only hint that "without the shedding of blood there is no remission of sin," but the promise is the same: what authority had forbidden, the authority of the leader now requires.[39] In the promise and performance of permitted blood-letting, fascism enacts the fusion between its fundamental conformism and its pseudo-revolutionary activism as a "movement." Second, the masochistic counterpoint to this sadistic other-directed aggression is a drive to self-destruction. For the fascist, "destruction [is] a substitute for his deepest and most inhibited desires . . . annihilation is the psychological substitute for the millennium."[40] In this spirit, Hitler promised (and delivered) "night and fog" to the nation which had failed him. Third, Adorno frequently draws attention to the *ritual* character of fascist, and particularly anti-Semitic, violence: "at the hub of the fascist, anti-Semitic, propaganda ritual is the desire for ritual murder."[41] The ritual element serves a number of functions. Most obviously, it connects with the syncretic paraphernalia of uniforms, insignia, oaths of loyalty and initiation rites which served to bind the follower to the Nazi "movement." The syndrome is re-enacted by those criminal gangs for whom the commission of murder is a final initiation rite. At a deeper psychodynamic level the ritual elements of fascist aggression are "simply the organised imitation of magic practices, the mimesis of mimesis."[42] Here, the element of pretense, of an acting

9

out which is not altogether real fuses with the notion of ritual as a sanctioned expression of affect. Reasserting his dominant theme, Adorno insists that "this loosening of self control, the merging of one's impulses with a ritual scheme is closely related to the universal psychological weakening of the self-contained individual."[43]

DEPENDENCE AND CONFORMITY: LINKING FASCISM AND THE CULTURE INDUSTRY

For Adorno the prejudice, aggression and conformism of fascism could not be dismissed as a heteronomous intrusion into the otherwise civilized order of modern society. On the contrary, fascism is at home in capitalist modernity. If it is a form of "irrationalism" its roots are none the less also those of what now passes for "reason." It was because he saw fascism as a possibility built into the very fabric of modern capitalism that Adorno was muted in his celebration of the defeat of its Italian and German manifestations. To state the case crudely, Adorno saw the commodified American culture of mass-consumption, movies, jazz and radio serials as putting into play the same basic psychodynamic principles that formed the basis of fascism: psychological dependency and social conformism. The homologies between fascism and the culture industry can be explored in a discussion of three themes which are common to "The Stars Down to Earth" and "Anti-Semitism and Fascist Propaganda." They can be labeled "the rhetoric of dependency," "seriousness and unseriousness" and "rationality and irrationality."

The Rhetoric of Dependency

When Adorno made a study of radio broadcasts by the anti-Semitic preacher Martin Luther Thomas and compared them to other similar materials he was struck by "the amazing stereotypy of all the fascist propaganda material known to us," observing that the "cliches" or "devices" employed by fascist agitators "could be boiled down to no more than thirty formulas."[44] The rather loose structure of the "Thomas" study consists of discussions of thirty-four such "devices" assembled in four larger groups. The first group of devices concerns the "self-characterization" of the agitator. For example:

"Lone Wolf": "I have no sponsors, and no politicians ever put one dollar into this movement."

"Persecuted Innocence": "they write everything against me, they

10

write that they are going to kill me."

"Indefatigability": "I am asking you only to sacrifice with me. I don't ask you to work as hard as I work."[45]

In the second group of devices Adorno identifies what he takes to be the kernel of "Thomas's method," in the third he examines the specifically "religious" dimension of Thomas's propaganda and in the fourth he lists the political topics which Thomas most frequently uses as "ideological bait." For Adorno, the stereotypy of these devices is itself a psychologically well-judged ploy which he sees reflected in the wider culture industry and the ritual element of fascism: "the prospective fascist follower craves this rigid repetition, just as the jitterbug craves the standard pattern of popular song . . . Mechanical application of these patterns is one of the essentials of the ritual."[46]

Beyond this, Adorno documents the way in which each device sets off a series of psychological resonances which will further bind the vulnerable listener to Thomas's "movement." Many of these resonances have already been discussed in general terms. The "listen to your leader" device veils the emptiness of the Führer principle in a "fetish" akin to the principle of all advertising slogans. The "tingling backbone" device alludes to the atrocities committed by the enemy to mobilize the sado-masochistic ambivalence of authoritarianism. The "great little man" device portrays the leader as the mixture of "pettiness and grandeur"[47] which encourages two levels of narcissistic identification (with the suburban barber and King Kong). One particular device, or rather a collection of devices which Adorno terms the *"fait accompli* technique," is of particular interest because of its closeness to the theme of "Stars." The psychological appeal of many specific rhetorical devices turns on "presenting an issue as one that previously has been decided."[48] In fascist propaganda the movement has unstoppable momentum, the leader has unconquerable strength, and a final blood thirsty settling of accounts with the enemy is inevitable. The technique has many superficial attractions: people want to be associated with a successful concern and are likely to think twice before opposing it. However, the technique has an objective basis in the fact that "to most people their life actually *is* decided in advance." By resonating with this experience "the *fait accompli* technique . . . touches upon one of the central mechanisms of the mass psychology of fascism: the transformation of one's feeling of one's own impotence into a feeling of strength."[49] That feeling arises "mysteriously and irrationally" from the acknowledgement of weakness and identification with the victor.

As an afterthought, Adorno adds "by the way" that the same mechanism is activated "throughout modern mass culture, particularly in the cinema."[50] The promotion and manipulation of fatalism is a central theme of "Stars." Caroll Righter's "Astrological Forecasts" column

> indulges in a symbolic expression and psychological fortification of the pressure that is being continuously exercised upon people. They are simply to have faith in that which is anyway . . . they are trained to identify themselves with the existent *in abstracto* rather than with heroic persons, to concede their own impotence, and are thereby allowed as a compensation to go on living without too much worrying.[51]

The trade-off to which Adorno alludes here is the formula for a quiet life of dependency and conformism that is as appropriate to "getting by" in the consumerist United States as in Nazi Germany.

Adorno arrives at the most basic rhetorical principle of Righter's column by noting a powerful obstacle to its aim, which he takes to be "promoting conventional, conformist and contented attitudes."[52] The obstacle is simply that people "find out from everyday life experience . . . that everything does not run so smooth as the column seems to imply it does and that not everything takes care of itself."[53] The column's readers will experience life as making *contradictory* demands of them, and as Adorno notes, "the column has to take up these contradictions themselves if it really wants to tie the readers to its own authority."[54] Adorno observes that the majority of "forecasts" in the column recommend different activities for different times of day, the chief division being between "A.M." and "P.M.". In short, "the problem of how to dispense with contradictory requirements of life is solved by the simple device of distributing these requirements over different periods mostly of the same day."[55]

In this "bi-phasic" approach, A.M. is for work, reality and the ego principle. P.M. is *apparently* for "the instinctual urges of the pleasure principle."[56] The qualification is required for two related reasons. First, the "pleasures" of P.M. are clearly subordinated in the column to the requirements of A.M.: pleasure is a reward or a compensation for work. Second, pleasure is only permissible "if it serves ultimately some ulterior purpose of success and self-promotion,"[57] so that eventually pleasure itself becomes a duty, a form of work. In the psychoanalytic literature, as Adorno points out, bi-phasic behavior is a symptom of compulsive neurosis. He cites Fenichel's observation that in bi-phasic behavior "the patient behaves alternately as though he were a naughty child and a strict punitive disciplinarian."[58] This neurotic pattern structures many of the rhetorical devices of the astrology column and of fascist propaganda: weakness and strength, masochism and sadism, conformity and rebellion, social forces and individuality, conservatism and modernism. The reader or listener is offered not a resolution of contradiction but its quasi-neurotic enactment in a regulated oscillation between the two poles, an oscillation in which the pole of weakness, masochism, conformity and abstract social force is dominant.

Two rhetorical consequences flow from this bi-phasic structure. First, and most obviously in the case of fascist agitators such as Thomas, it is a mistake to look for *arguments* in such material: "in objective terms, Thomas's radio speeches are quite illogical."[59] But this matters no more than it matters that the neurotic's compulsions are "illogical": fascist propaganda, and by analogy the wider culture, is obedient only to the "logic" of the unconscious. Second, the rhetorical task is to present behavior which reinforces weakness, masochism and conformity as if it were its opposite. Righter's recommendations for A.M. frequently focus on the reader's relationship with superiors at work, or "higher-ups," while the key relationships in P.M. are with friends and family. Each category functions, for Adorno, as an embodiment of the demands of society in the different spheres of life. He cites many examples of the tenor of Righter's view of relationships.

Influential friend gives good pointer for securing wish, goal . . . Executive or responsible higher-up, if contacted by you will show right way to increase and expand present outlets . . . A powerful man readily gives you a bright new course of action if you evidence interest.[60]

In each case, the trick is to present psychological dependency and social conformity as a cleverly-judged individual strategy of self-advancement that at the same time does away with the need for any real choice. "An attempt is made to transform narcissistic losses into the gain of getting rid of the burden of autonomous responsibility and, possibly, adding some masochistic gratifications."[61]

As usual, Adorno insists on the ubiquity of this mechanism within modern culture: conformity is the socially sanctioned form of "self-expression." If Righter's column (and by implication the wider culture) differ from straightforward propaganda it is because the column is subject to a kind of "censorship." For example, Adorno asks "why so much is made of the friends while little or nothing is made of the foes," giving only half of an incipiently paranoid bi-phasic opposition.[62] Earlier he notes that references to threats to the reader are almost always couched in a euphemism:

> one of the most widely spread realistic threats, that of being fired, appears only in a diluted form, e.g. as conflicts with higher-ups, being "dressed down," and similar unpleasantnesses. The term "firing" is not used a single time.[63]

While Adorno does not discuss the issue explicitly, the underlying model is of a rhetorical and psychological continuum from the "everyday" products of the culture industry through quasi-propaganda such as Righter's column to frank fascist agitation. Adorno makes it clear in "Thomas," for example, that while Thomas's radio broadcasts are relatively subdued and euphemistic, his "live" addresses to his followers "could whip [the audience] up to the peak of emotional hatred. Here alone his anti-Semitic propaganda went unchecked."[64] The "exoteric" radio speeches are to be understood as advertising (and fund-raising) for the more virulent "esoteric" movement. The source of Adorno's pessimism about the threat of fascism is his conviction that the rantings of a Thomas or a Hitler play on the same regressed character structure as do soap operas and astrology columns. The rhetoric of fascist propaganda is simply a less censored version of the ubiquitous rhetoric of the culture industry.

Seriousness and unseriousness

While its effects might be deadly, fascist propaganda is not altogether "serious." Fascist agitators do not present their audiences with considered lectures on the shortcomings of the democratic theory of the state, or even with exhortatory sermons in the traditional sense. The audience who turn out to see and hear the fascist agitator expect a good show. For Adorno "show" is indeed the right word. The achievement of the self-styled leader is a performance reminiscent of the theater, of sport, and of so-called religious revivals."[65] Their "sentimentality, blatant insincerity and phoniness"[66] are not flaws in such performances, but the core of their appeal. The showman-like fakery of the agitator links him to the snake-oil salesman, the circus performer and an entire tradition of folk art marked by "a very strong tendency toward exaggerated sentimentality and 'false tones.'"[67] It is the element of performance which accounts for the "hundreds and hundreds of pages of purest nonsense which one can find in Thomas', and it might be added, in Hitler's uncensored speeches."[68] The content does not matter, the "show" consists of the agitator's glibness, his "mysterious gift of speech" manifested in a mixture of "maudlin ecstasy and senseless chatter."[69]

It follows from this diagnosis that many of the agitator's rhetorical devices can succeed even while their audience regards them as something of a joke. An analogy might be drawn with advertising campaigns which make self-evidently absurd claims or show impossible physical transformations. As Jhally has remarked in an analysis which draws on Adorno's work, advertising is "a discourse where all normal physical and social arrangements are held in abeyance."[70] We regard the claims as joke, but we buy the products not in spite of, but because of, the joke. So it may be with fascist propaganda. For example, the "persecuted innocence" device (see above) serves as a useful rationale for the persecution of the alleged persecutors, be they the communists, the Jews or the Poles. The perception that such uses are somewhat contrived or cynical need not detract from their success. Indeed, people might enjoy a chuckle about the cunning of their fascist leaders. As Adorno writes, "in Germany the 'persecuted innocence' device always was used with a certain cynicism and was received as such. For example, innumerable jokes of the type 'Jew peddler bites Aryan shepherd dog' were enjoyed."[71]

The strain of unseriousness which Bernstein has termed "seeing through and obeying"[72] extends to the case of astrology: few people would confess to reading a newspaper or magazine astrology column for anything other than amusement. The unseriousness of the astrology column is linked to its status as a "secondary superstition." As Adorno observes, "the occult as such plays only a marginal role" in contemporary astrology, where it is "institutionalized, objectified and, to a large extent, socialized."[73] Astrology is a "secondary superstition" on an analogy with the "secondary community" where "people are related to each other [only] through intermediary objectified social processes (e.g., exchange of commodities)."[74] Adorno goes on to link the "abstractness" of modern astrology, which derives from its tenuous link to the occult, with an "absence of ultimate 'seriousness'".[75]

However, and as Adorno points out elsewhere, the "seriousness" of *all* modern occultism is problematic. In "Theses Against Occultism" it is portrayed as a function of the "fetishism of commodities:" "menacingly objectified labour assails [the occultist] on all sides from demonically grimacing objects."[76] In its relation to commodification, and in the homologies between occult and totalitarian terror, occultism is eminently modern. "By its regression to magic under late capitalism, thought is assimilated to late capitalist forms."[77] It represents an impossible attempt to recover a sense of the "objective" meaning of events in a world where

15

all meaning is attenuated and subjectivized, an attempt whose results can only be absurd and disturbing. Occultism is "an unconscious compulsive projection of a subject decomposing historically if not clinically."[78]

If the unseriousness of fascist propaganda has a considerable element of joking and showmanship, the unseriousness of the secondary, minimalist, occultism of Righter's column is more directly cognitive. People may not "believe in" astrology, but then they are not required to "believe in" anything much in late modern society. The fact that people do not "believe in" astrology no more prevents them from attending to Righter's column than the fact that they do not "believe in" advertising prevents them from functioning as consumers. At this point the problem of "unseriousness" begins to mutate into the problem of rationality and irrationality in fascism, astrology and the wider culture.

Rationality and irrationality

Adorno hesitates to characterize fascist propaganda as simply "irrational." As he puts it, "the term, irrationality, is much too vague to describe sufficiently so complex a psychological phenomenon."[79] However, his own views on the complex interplay of the rational and irrational in his material are not entirely worked out. Rather, a number of different themes emerge at different points in the texts. Of course, this observation is not necessarily a criticism of Adorno, for whom it would be distortion wholly typical of "identity thinking" to attempt to capture so ambivalent a phenomenon as fascist propaganda under a single, self-consistent, concept.

Perhaps the most overtly rationalistic model to attract Adorno is that of fascism as a "racket" (in the American sense), an approach made famous in Brecht's *The Resistible Rise of Arturo Ui*.

> The assertion that fascist organizations like Thomas's Crusade are rackets is to be taken very seriously. It does not refer merely to the habitual participation of criminals in such movements, nor to their violent terroristic practices. It emphasizes their sociological structure as such: they are repressive, exclusive and more or less secret ingroups.[80]

It is the debunking function of the term "racket" which appeals to Adorno: fascism loses its glamour and mystique if it is "just another racket." Thus, the frequent attacks which Thomas makes on established politics as a racket of the communists and Jews is a transparent defensive trick. "Fewer, he reasons, will believe him a racketeer, if he thus violently attacks racketeering."[81]

16

More important to Adorno than the debunking of "fascism-as-a-racket" is the more complex analysis of fascist propaganda as a form of psychological manipulation. In a formula for the ambivalent rationality–irrationality of fascism, he states that "the irrational gratifications which fascism offers are themselves planned and handled in an utterly rational way."[82] He coins the term "psycho-technics" to label this form of manipulation, going on to assert that "Thomas' radio speeches offer an excellent example for one of the basic characteristics of fascist and anti-Semitic propaganda, namely, the entirely calculated, highly rationalistic nature of its irrationalism."[83] But Adorno can give no account of the knowledge-base from which this rationalistic calculation proceeds beyond a certain common-sense shrewdness. A Hitler or a Thomas may know that their "maudlin ecstasy and senseless chatter" will have the desired effect, but it is less clear that every performance is "entirely calculated." Adorno himself is a little uneasy on this point. Immediately before the passage quoted above he concedes that "a certain affinity between the speaker's mind and the supposed muddle-headedness of his listeners should not be discounted." Later, reflecting on Thomas's very effective oscillation between the high-flown and the mundane, he remarks that it is "hard to say" whether the technique "is entirely conscious with Thomas, or whether it is due to his actually representing an average lower middle class type."[84] It may be that the most effective resolution of the paradox lies in the model of the popular performer and showground huckster discussed above. In a neat formula, "the fascist agitator is usually a masterly salesman of his own psychological defects."[85]

The gratifications which fascism provides are "irrational" for Adorno because they are illusory: "there is no real pleasure or joy, but only the release of one's own feeling of unhappiness."[86] However, and as Adorno the Freudian also recognizes, from the standpoint of the psychic economy these "irrational" gratifications have their own "rationality." They make the best of a bad job in the same way as do neurotic symptoms.

The category of "paranoia," which was discussed in general terms in the previous section, is mobilized by Adorno in both "Thomas" and "Stars" to contain the troublesome ambivalence of rationality–irrationality. In the more theoretical "Stars" the issue is discussed explicitly. Writing of astrological magazines rather than Righter's column, Adorno notes the "pseudo-rationality" of astrology which distances it from the "lunatic fringe" of occultism.[87] Its appeal, like that of other paranoid projections, is founded in a climate of "semi-erudition."

17

Astrology, just as other irrational creeds such as racism, provides a short cut by bringing the complex to a handy formula and offering at the same time the pleasant gratification that he who feels to be excluded from educational privileges nevertheless belongs to the minority of those who are "in the know." [88]

At the end of "Stars" Adorno positions astrology with fascism as responses to a sense of dependence which arises as people perceive their worlds

more as a "system" than ever before, covered by an all-comprising net of organization with no loopholes where the individual could "hide" . . . It is this reality situation which has so many and obvious similarities with paranoid systems of thinking that it seems to invite such patterns.[89]

When social "reality" models itself after a paranoid system, paranoid thinking is an eminently "rational" response.

DOES ADORNO STILL MATTER?

Adorno's twin theses that, first, authoritarian irrationalism lies at the core of enlightened modernity and that, second, the culture industry is implicated in authoritarian irrationalism have a legitimate claim on the attention of students of contemporary culture. In elaborating the nature and extent of that claim, two extremes need to be avoided. First, and most familiar (see below), is the self-satisfied dismissal of Adorno as an unnecessarily gloomy and elitist dead German whose preoccupations might be understandable in biographical terms, but which "we" have left behind. However, it would do no service to Adorno's conception of the critical analysis of culture to turn him into a public monument from which the pigeon droppings of mis-interpretation and mis-use must be ritually removed: there should be no "Adornoism." The nature and extent of Adorno's claim to attention must always be contingent on the degree to which his work can illuminate contemporary developments in culture, polity and society. The starting point for any assessment along these lines must be a clear sense of Adorno's flaws and limitations. More positively, an assessment must identify core themes in Adorno's analysis which continue to merit attention and to warrant further development.

Problems of method

It is perhaps best to begin with the most problematic issue. Adorno

18

possessed an unusually acute sense of the gravitational pull exerted by "identity thinking" in the study of culture.[90] "Theses Against Occultism" exemplifies the density and subtlety of Adorno's essayistic, aphoristic, writing. However, he was much less comfortable with empirical methods of analysis and his discomfort leaves its mark on both "Stars" and the "Thomas" study. Paradoxically for an analyst of eminently "rhetorical" materials, speech and writing which sets out to persuade an audience, Adorno is not very interested in "rhetoric" as such. To put it another way, his is a psychodynamic model of rhetoric in which the persuasive force of language lies in its capacity to resonate with the psychological needs of audiences.

The approach is spelled out in a rather peremptory way in the introduction to "Stars": "we want to give a picture of the specific stimuli operating on followers of astrology . . . and of the presumptive effects of these stimuli."[91] The operative and problematic term is "presumptive." While the methodology of the "Thomas" study is not discussed by Adorno, it clearly rests on the same assumptions as that of "Stars." Adorno writes confidently of "the emotional needs of the group to which [Thomas] addresses himself" purely on the basis of Thomas's addresses.[92] In "Stars," while Adorno seems to regret the lack of opportunity for "real field work" he does not regard this as an obstacle to presenting the study of Righter's column as "an attempt to understand what astrological publications mean in terms of reader reactions."[93]

In fine, "Stars" and the "Thomas" study share a double methodological flaw in which rhetorical materials are treated as windows on the psychology of their audience, and the psychology of the audience is "read off" from rhetorical materials. In addition, there is little evidence of any systematic sampling technique in "Stars" particularly: extracts from the column have been selected to illustrate themes whose representative character is not established. These are not simply naive errors on Adorno's part, of course. They can be traced to a suspicion of the American empirical tradition of audience research which Adorno's failed collaboration with Lazarsfeld exacerbated. He came to believe that such research isolated a single moment of subjective response from the objective totality while privileging the conscious over the unconscious reaction.[94]

These methodological difficulties do not negate the interest and topicality of the two studies, but they do call into question the degree of empirical backing which Adorno can claim for his arguments, particularly as they relate to audiences, and they do problematize the claim of the studies to be procedural models for contemporary analysis.

The best case for Adorno's "audience" analysis lies in its convergence with some of the concerns of "Reader-Response" criticism. Adorno may not be able to claim knowledge of the flesh and blood audience persons who read Righter's column or listen to Thomas's addresses, but he can and does study the "imagined readers" or "narratees" projected by the texts which make available preferred audience positions for readers and listeners.[95]

However, this analogy draws attention again to Adorno's displacement of rhetoric as it is fused with psychodynamic processes. One way forward may lie with the "rhetorical" re-casting of social psychology advocated by Billig, who insists that we understand "attitudes" as "stances on matters of public debate" constituted in the context of ongoing argument, of "criticism and justification."[96] If a person has "anti-Semitic attitudes," for example, those attitudes can be formed only in and from the discursive stuff of debate pro and con anti-Semitism. On this basis a bi-phasic dissonance between general attitudes (anti-Semitism) and specific behaviors (kindness to an individual Jew) may reflect nothing more than the difference between two discursive-rhetorical contexts which are not fused together. Adorno assumes that since the bi-phasic oppositions of fascist propaganda are logically contradictory, they must be rooted in psychodynamic principles. However, from a rhetorical perspective, argument is always and everywhere bi-phasic: rhetoric moves between the poles of an argument with a persuasive force that is neither logical nor wholly unconscious. In a discussion of prejudice Billig criticizes the way in which *The Authoritarian Personality* interprets as no more than "lip service" to community standards those qualifications made by respondents to their "prejudiced" statements.[97] Billig argues that prejudice is argumentative and that prejudiced persons often display considerable argumentative, or rhetorical, subtlety.

On this kind of analysis the struggle against authoritarian irrationalism in all its variants involves a battle for rhetorical command of the "common places" of everyday discourse which embody taken-for-granted moral and political assumptions. One might say that the danger posed by fascist propaganda, by the 'devices' documented by Adorno, is two-fold. When the common places of a culture are predominantly liberal, fascism most obviously offers "arguments" for over-riding them, but it also plants words, phrases, jokes which have the potential to "colonize" everyday life itself. It follows that the spirit of Adorno's project for a critical theory of authoritarianism and its relationship with the wider culture requires a closer attention than he himself gave to the rhetorical, persuasive, dimension of authoritarian discourse.

Freudianism

Adorno's Freudianism is involved in his most penetrating insights but, as has already been seen, it raises considerable difficulties. Freudianism is under sustained assault from many quarters: as modernist meta-narrative, as masculinism and as pseudo-science. Any full assessment would have to begin by placing Adorno's psychoanalytic account of fascist propaganda and the wider syndrome of dependency in the context of a wider debate which involved his radical Freudian contemporaries. Adorno was far from the only "Freudo-Marxist" intellectual of his generation to attempt critical accounts of fascism and American consumer culture. Without exploring finer points of doctrine, a comparison between Adorno and Reich on the one hand and Marcuse on the other reveals some interesting lacunae.[98]

The comparison demonstrates, first, the extent to which Adorno was blind to gender issues and to questions of sexuality. For all his insistence on the "libidinal" character of the tie between fascist leader and follower he does not explore the most obvious questions about the implication of gendered forms of eroticism in fascist politics (beyond a few passing references to ties between sado-masochism and male homosexuality). Second, the same comparison reveals the weakness of Adorno's proposed propaganda response to fascist agitation. Having demonstrated over and again the extraordinary power of fascist manipulation of the unconscious, all Adorno can suggest by way of response is that various contradictions and absurdities should be "pointed out" to the population at risk.[99] Reich's advocacy of frequent and vigorous heterosexual intercourse as a prophylactic against the blandishments of fascism, or Marcuse's (much later) advocacy of "polymorphous perversity" may have been eccentric, but at least they attempted to match the libidinal effects of authoritarianism and one-dimensional consumerism on their own ground.

If Adorno's particular variant of Freudianism is problematic for some critics, any sort of Freudianism is a problem for mainstream Anglophone social psychology. Despite the interest excited by *The Authoritarian Personality*, and partly because of that work's perceived methodological weakness, psychodynamic accounts of fascism quite soon shrank to a small part of multi-dimensional accounts, notably under the influence of Allport.[100] Important studies of racist prejudice in Britain have adopted Allport's pluralism,[101] while Altemeyer has more recently re-covered the ground of *The Authoritarian Personality* from a social learning perspective.[102] For many people working in the field, psychoanalytic explanations of fascism are either insufficiently wide-ranging or insufficiently parsimonious to merit very much attention.

So, how indispensable is an acceptance of Freudian theory to a sympathetic reading of Adorno's account of authoritarian irrationalism? To state the case dogmatically, little sense can be made of Adorno without reference to three axioms. First, the "character" of the human individual is the dynamic product of a life-history which is, in turn, shaped by broader social and cultural influences. Second, character structure has "depth" in the sense that its complex dynamics are not fully present to self-consciousness. Third, the "unconscious" dimensions of character are implicated in the ways human individuals orient themselves to social interactions and cultural meanings. If these axioms are rejected, little sense can be made of Adorno's two major hypotheses: that first, social and cultural developments in late capitalism produce typically "weak" character structures with high dependency needs and that second, those dependency needs are routinely manipulated by diverse interests, from fascist agitators to commercial advertisers.

However, while there is no doubt that Adorno regarded Freudian theory as the most highly developed framework in which to articulate those axioms and hypotheses, it need not be regarded as the only possible one. This is another way of saying that Adorno's analyses of the psycho-dynamics of fascism and the culture industry do not automatically collapse even if it is granted that Freudianism is discredited. His hypotheses could be articulated, and made available for investigation, in a number of other discourses of the human subject, from interactionist social psychology to postmodernist culture theory.[103]

Anti-Semitism and fascism

The question of the relevance of Adorno's focus on anti-Semitism has already been touched upon. Anti-Semitism lives on, even if it is over-shadowed by more popular forms of prejudice. As Billig writes of British fascism:

> anti-Semitism is no longer a major recruiting force; anti-black prejudice would be a much more satisfactory criterion for potential fascism in Britain. Yet, the peculiar nature of the fascist tradition ensures that anti-Semitism still retains an important ideological function. Its role may be less connected with the outward appeals of propaganda . . . and more to do with the ideology and practice of the fascist élite.[104]

If this shift requires some re-assessment of the emphasis Adorno places on anti-Semitism, in one respect it emphasizes Adorno's relevance. The appeal of anti-Semitism to insiders is its status as the "secret" which explains everything and is available only to initiates. Like occultism and astrology, anti-Semitism is a paranoid projection of the "semi-erudite." A rather more root-and-branch critique of Adorno is implied in Bauman's important reflections on the Holocaust. Bauman asserts the "modernity" of the Holocaust in two senses. First, he argues that anti-Semitic "racism" of the Nazi type is to be distinguished from the common run of "heterophobia" and regarded as a science-based form of social engineering.[105] Second, Bauman argues persuasively that the Holocaust was made possible by the convergence of "normal" features of institutionalized modernity: bureaucratic organization, the erosion of ethical by technical rationality and the micro-dynamics of obedience to authority.[106] Rather in passing, Bauman offers a caricature in which "Adorno's vision divided the world into born proto-Nazis and their victims" and asserts that Adorno advanced the comforting thesis that "the explanation of Nazi rule and ensuing atrocities [lay] in the presence of a special type of individual."[107]

A defence of Adorno can begin with what has been seen as a limitation of *The Authoritarian Personality*: "no actual fascists were studied."[108] This explains why Adorno and his colleagues regarded their findings as far from "comforting," because characterological susceptibility to the blandishments of fascism was precisely *not* confined to a few easily identified German "proto-Nazis." In fact, Adorno's concerns and Bauman's are distinct and complementary. While the Holocaust gave Adorno's work its point and urgency, it is not his actual object of analysis. Neither is he directly concerned with the mechanics of fascist rule. Adorno's concern, rather, is with the way fascist propaganda works, the threat it poses, in democratic societies. If a parallel is sought between Adorno's American-based studies and the German experience, it surely relates to the Weimar period, to the ways in which agitation and propaganda were able to mobilize enough support to bring the Nazis to power. Bauman has as little to say about this process as Adorno has to say about the mechanics of extermination. Viewed in this way, Adorno's account of the modernity of authoritarian irrationalism is a powerful and disturbing complement to Bauman's account of the modernity of the Holocaust.

Change and popular culture

The case that Adorno has been unjustly neglected by mainstream cultural studies is not new. Harris, for example, has provided a telling account of the way the "Gramscian" tradition lacked

23

an account of the modern culture industry or surveillance apparatuses, and their capacity to fight back by incorporating critics and inverting their work. This account goes missing partly because of the early decision to reject "mass culture theses," and to construct a caricature out of Adorno's and Horkheimer's version.[109]

North American cultural studies have been rather more receptive to his work than the British variant, as the Angus and Jhally collection bears witness.[110] Overall, however, Adorno's star has waned. In a curious irony his theologically inclined protégé Walter Benjamin was taken up as a more appropriate model for a "materialist" culture theory, while more recently the soviet literary critic and linguist Mikhail Bakhtin has acquired cult status. A reaction to the naiveties of Benjamin's celebration of the anti-auratic potential of popular culture and of a Bakhtin-inspired prole cult has begun in a few quarters, and Adorno's work has an important contribution to make here.

It is notable and regrettable that McGuigan's otherwise impressive critique of "populism" shares the attitude of the populists themselves towards Adorno's work. He urges a rapprochement between cultural studies and "the political economy of culture" as a hedge against the populist drift.[111] At least part of Adorno's importance lies in the question mark which he places against a conventional political-economic approach to culture. Angus and Jhally formulate the two major points. First, late capitalist culture has "attained a measure of autonomy and also importance to the survival of the whole social system." Second, in these circumstances "it is no longer so much the question of determination by the economy that is important, but rather the imposition of the 'commodity form' on cultural productions."[112]

Among the charges routinely leveled against Adorno two, particularly, merit attention here. First, Adorno is held to treat cultural consumers as passive "dopes." This stance detracts attention from the complexities of audience activity, and amounts to "a-taken-for-grantedly demeaning view of ordinary people's tastes and pleasures," as McGuigan put it.[113] Despite the shortcomings of Adorno's audience analysis discussed above, the "cultural dopes" interpretation is a subtle but significant distortion of his views. "Stars," for example, shows that Adorno can readily allow – even require – that readers "actively" make sense of Righter's column, relating its content to their own lives or circumstances. Equally, the audiences for Thomas's anti-Semitic ravings must "actively" come to the view that the Jews do, indeed, have a lot to answer for.

24

The critical point is simply that the "sense" people make is rarely within their entirely conscious control: sense-making puts into play a complex of background assumptions and motivations. Adorno's case is that the messages of propaganda and commodified culture work by resonating with those background factors so that the "sense" which is made will typically tend towards dependency and conformism. To put it another way, for Adorno it would be a stupendous analytic naivety to take anyone's "tastes and pleasures" at face-value as a simple datum.[114] It is surely possible to preserve Adorno's basic insight here without agreeing with every tendentious judgement he makes about popular genres.

A second important charge is that Adorno's vision of the culture industry and its effects lays too much stress on its monopolistic tendencies and on the homogeneity of its products. This vision seems particularly inappropriate to processes of postmodernizing change. As Bernstein notes, diversity is now the watchword of marketing and of popular culture.[115] One response to this development which would preserve the salience of Adorno's analysis is to argue that the diversity of market-segmentation and the cultivation of "lifestyle" is entirely bogus, a death mask of individuality covering the bland features of the "consumer clone."[116] A more interesting possibility may be to concede that Adorno was wrong in projecting a continuing homogenization of culture, but to explore the implications of his mistake with his own analytic resources.

In this spirit Jameson has asserted Adorno's relevance on the basis that his "introspective or reflexive dialectic befits a situation in which . . . the relationship between the individual and the system seems ill-defined, if not fluid, or even dissolved."[117] Bernstein also insists on Adorno's relevance to the study of a commodified culture of "lifestyles," in which a superficial "aestheticization of social reality," a "closing of the gap between the culture industry and everyday life," fails to accomplish any "true overcoming of the repressions of the work ethic" and thus "releases aggression in at least equal measure to its release of desire."[118] Adorno's studies of authoritarian irrationalism can address these fundamental questions about the fate of the self and the sources of aggression which have reappeared on the agenda of postmodernizing cultures. However, a category which may be of even more significance than "aggression" is "dependency."

An important dimension of the fluidity of contemporary culture lies in the apparent necessity for constant and individualized choice in a world where traditional social determinants of taste and belief have lost their binding force, and where a bewildering diversity of goods, services and opinions are constantly on display. It may be that for characters formed after the demise of the "psychological corner shop" the necessity for even a relatively trivial "lifestyle" choice must be both attractive and threatening. Lifestyle magazines and television programs, consumer guides of all kinds and advertising itself might be analyzed as responses to the panic of dependent personalities faced with choices they are not equipped to make alone. Perhaps the consumer guide is the contemporary equivalent to Righter's astrological column, but one which recognizes that conformity must now be accommodated within diversity.

Adorno himself draws attention to the role which the provision of "information" plays in the workings of the culture industry, in its "high" as well as "low" niches.

> If mass culture has already become one great exhibition, then everyone who stumbles into it feels as lonely as a stranger on an exhibition site. This is where information leaps in. The endless exhibition is also the endless bureau of information, which forces itself on the hapless visitor and regales him with leaflets, guides and radio recommendations, sparing each individual from the disgrace of appearing as stupid as everyone else.[119]

Postmodernizing change might be seen as intensifying, rather than relaxing, pressures towards dependency and conformism through the demand for information. After all, the successful adoption of a lifestyle is only possible, only recognizable as such, on the basis of conformity. It may be that even contemporary fascist propaganda shares the condition of the consumer guide as a provider of instructions for successful lifestyle choice.

This possibility illuminates a number of cultural peculiarities of contemporary "neo-" fascism which seem to echo other of Adorno's themes. Even more than their originals, recent European fascisms are highly syncretic. German fascist youths parade in the costumes of British skinheads while carrying banners which imitate the swastika flag: theirs is a pastiche of fascism, but none the less dangerous for that. They have made what may well be a somewhat distracted choice of fascism, but they don't yet quite know how to be fascists. This element of not entirely convincing pastiche brings to mind Adorno's remarks on the element of "unseriousness" in fascist propaganda. While their thugs mill rather self-consciously in the streets, the besuited leaders of the new movement offer television cameras their versions of the "democratic cloak" and "persecuted innocence" devices, not expecting or intending to be taken wholly seriously. In Italy, the most famous fascist politician is a woman who is a descendant of Mussolini and a relative of Sophia Loren. She features frequently and prominently in the "glossies." there, fascism converges with the entertainment industry and the cult of the "leader" converges with the personality fetish of popular magazines.

A further unsettling range of postmodernizing possibilities relates to Adorno's account of the links between pseudo-rationality, paranoia and authoritarianism. While paranoia has been consigned to the modern side of the modern–postmodern divide in at least one influential account,[120] there are grounds for regarding paranoid projection as linked to postmodernizing change. The paranoid character of many *fin de siècle* concerns about health and the environment is really quite marked: our brains will turn to blancmange if we eat beef, power lines will give us cancer, we will be boiled by global warming or fried by ultra-violet light. Of course, the old adage holds that "just because you're paranoid it doesn't mean they're not out to get you," and our fears may be well-grounded. It is not the "scientific" basis of health and environmental panics which is at issue here so much as the way in which they are generated by forms of media coverage which might be regarded as encouraging paranoid thinking among the scientifically "semi-erudite." This issue connects with Adorno's notorious disparagement of phenomena from soap opera and jazz to astrology, vegetarianism and natural healing which are today intrinsic parts of "popular" or "alternative" cultures regarded benignly by most progressive students of culture. Might progressive culture and politics also have a paranoid and authoritarian underside?

The challenge which Adorno's work on authoritarianism poses here is one which he did not take up himself. Contemporary critics of *The Authoritarian Personality* such as Shils asked why it was simply assumed that pathological authoritarianism was a characteristic of the political right and not the statist, collectivist left.[121] It is an entirely unquestioned assumption of the texts collected here that while political error is grounded in psychopathology, political correctness can flow only from psychic health. It is curious, given Adorno's numerous debts to Nietzsche that this assumption seems to ignore Nietzsche's warning that we should not assume that truth corresponds to human purposes. The challenge is surely to ask directly whether cultural activities and political movements of which we approve might not be driven, in part, by the same principles as are those of which we disapprove. It must be an open question whether, say, environmentalism might share rhetorical and psycho-dynamic features with forms of right-wing authoritarianism, whether the two might have a certain formal equivalence in a postmodernizing culture which merges politics with lifestyle choice.

The question of "paranoid" thinking arises here once more. Contemporary authoritarian propaganda (and not only from the extra-parliamentary right) might be thought to display two features which Baudrillard identifies in contemporary (post)culture. First, authoritarianism has the air of a panic production: its elements of syncretic pastiche and nostalgia ('family," "nation," etc.) are a bid for cognitive reassurance in the face of a "loss of reality." Second, and in consequence, such propaganda simulates a meaningful and shared symbolic order. Baudrillard characterizes "simulation" in terms very close to those used by Adorno in relation to "paranoia": "a short-circuit of reality and its reduplication by signs."[122] Adorno's theme of bi-phasic ambivalence might find a place here, too: individuals might be conceived as moving in and out of simulations (family, work, sport, politics, etc.) that project systems of action and meaning which would be radically incommensurate if translated into a propositional form. On this basis a strong case can be made that rhetorical hypostatizations of "the market," "the family," "the nation" or indeed "the environment" as the bedrock reality should be understood as entering a register of paranoia-simulation.

So, to answer the question posed in the heading of this concluding section, Adorno *does* still matter. As was stated at the outset, it does no service to Adorno to try to defend every word of the essays collected here. An attempt has been made to indicate where some of the major problems lie. In the end, Adorno's work on authoritarian irrationalism matters because if we read it critically, but without reliance on those caricatures which have been so influential, it can raise profoundly unsettling questions about contemporary culture. To read these essays in that way is to ask how far dependency has become the typical condition of the "self" in advanced societies, how deeply authoritarian currents run through our superficially pluralistic cultures, and how free our beliefs and opinions are from a pervasive undercurrent of irrationalism.

NOTES TO THE INTRODUCTION

1 It was published anonymously in *Studies in Philosophy and Social Science* (9) under the general rubric "Institute Activities." The "Project" had been drafted and re-drafted since 1939 by Adorno and Max Horkheimer, with inputs from Leo Lowenthal and Franz Neumann (see R. Wiggershaus, *The Frankfurt School*. Cambridge: Polity Press, 1994, pp. 273–7).
2 T.W. Adorno, "The Psychological Technique of Martin Luther Thomas's Radio Addresses," *Gesammelte Schriften* (9.1). Frankfurt: Suhrkamp Verlag, 1975.
3 Perhaps one should write "fascist racism." However, the more general

expression is not simply a euphemism. First, as is suggested immediately below, Adorno himself argues that fascism and racism are the tip of the iceberg of a more general syndrome of authoritarianism and irrationalism. Second, as is discussed in the final section of this "Introduction," it is a moot point where the boundaries of that syndrome should be drawn. It is certainly not clear that it implicates only the extreme right of a political spectrum, for example.

4   "Research Project on Anti-Semitism," this volume, p. 135.

5   *The Independent*, London, 8 February 1994. The extremely bitter irony of this case is that the unfortunate Rohn was not Jewish, but claimed to be in order to "gain sympathy."

6   *The Guardian*, London, 28 January 1994.

7   Z. Bauman, *Modernity and the Holocaust*. Cambridge: Polity Press, 1989, pp. 39–41.

8   See M. Jay, "Anti-Semitism and the Weimar Left" in his *Permanent Exiles*. New York: Columbia University Press, 1985, p. 86.

9   The term "anti-Semitism" is inappropriate in many ways, as a formula such as "Palestinian anti-Semitism" shows. However, and as David Berger argues, it "has become so deeply entrenched that resistance to its use is probably futile." (D. Berger (ed.), *History and Hate: the Dimensions of anti-Semitism*. Philadelphia, the Jewish Publication Society, 1986, p. 1.)

10   K. Evans, "Radical time-bomb under British Islam," *The Guardian*, London, 7 February 1994. An inset to the same story contains extracts from Hibz ut Tahrir leaflets, with a reference to "the filth of occupying Jews" and a description of Western education systems as "Jew-designated mortuaries of wisdom."

11   "Research Project on Anti-Semitism," this volume, p. 135.

12   Ibid., p. 172.

13   Ibid.

14   M. Horkheimer, "Egoism and the Freedom Movement: On the Anthropology of the Bourgeois Era," *Telos* 54, 1982, pp. 10–60 (first published in 1936).

15   "Research Project on Anti-Semitism," this volume, p. 147.

16   T.W. Adorno and M. Horkheimer, "Elements of Anti-Semitism," in *Dialectic of Enlightenment*. London: Verso, 1979, pp. 176–9.

17   M. Jay, *The Dialectical Imagination: a History of the Frankfurt School and the Institute of Social Research 1923–1950*. London: Heinemann, 1973, p. 231.

18   T.W. Adorno and M. Horkheimer, *Dialectic of Enlightenment*, p. 189.

19   Ibid., p. 190.

20   Ibid., p. 195.

21   "Research Project on Anti-Semitism," this volume, pp. 152–5.

22   Ibid., p. 190.

23   Ibid. It has sometimes been claimed that Germany was one of the *least* anti-Semitic nations of Europe in the early years of the century, a claim refuted by T. Endelman ("Comparative Perspectives on Modern Anti-Semitism in the West," in D. Berger (ed.), *History and Hate*). M. Jay is highly sceptical of Franz Neumann's version of the argument applied to Weimar Germany (see "Anti-Semitism and the Weimar Left"). Neumann's view is echoed in this quote from the "Research Project."

24 For a discussion of Institute debates on these issues see M. Jay's "Anti-Semitism and the Weimar Left" and "The Jews and the Frankfurt School" in his *Permanent Exiles*. See also R. Wiggershaus, *The Frankfurt School*, ch. 4. Their own empirical work in Germany before their emigration should have given members of the Institute reasons to doubt the level of resistance to anti-Semitism.

25 T.W. Adorno *et al.*, *The Authoritarian Personality*. New York: Harper, 1950. The other four studies were N. Ackerman and M. Jahoda, *Anti-Semitism and Emotional Disorder*. New York: Harper, 1950; B. Bettleheim and M. Janowitz, *Dynamics of Prejudice*. New York: Harper, 1950; L. Lowenthal and N. Guterman, *Prophets of Deceit*. New York: Harper, 1949; P. Massing, *Rehearsal For Destruction*. New York: Harper, 1949. The latter is an historical account of pre-Nazi anti-Semitism in Germany rather than an empirically based study of the contemporary USA.

26 M.B. Smith, "Foreword" to B. Altemeyer, *Enemies of Freedom*. San Francisco: Josey Bass, 1988, p. xi. Smith is quoting here his own review of 38 years earlier (*Journal of Abnormal and Social Psychology* 45, 1950, p. 775 f.).

27 Institute of Social Research, *Studien über autorität und Familie*. Paris: Alcan, 1936.

28 T.W. Adorno, "Freudian Theory and the Pattern of Fascist Propaganda," in his *The Culture Industry: Selected Essays on Mass Culture* (ed. J. Bernstein). London: Routledge, 1991, p. 123. The idea that authoritarianism was sado-masochistic in character was introduced to the Institute's thinking by Erich Fromm in the 1930s (in *Studien über autorität und Familie*).

29 T.W. Adorno, "Freudian Theory and the Pattern of Fascist Propaganda," p. 134n.

30 T.W. Adorno and M. Horkheimer, *Dialectic of Enlightenment*, p. 203.

31 For Adorno these child-like traits correspond to the phases of ontogenesis identified by Freud. So, identification with the fascist leader is a regression to orality, sado-masochism is linked to anality, while narcissism is characteristic of the phallic phases.

32 Adorno and Horkheimer are aware of the danger of making a fetish of the autonomous, Stoic bourgeois individual of competitive capitalism. As they wrote in "The Culture Industry: Enlightenment as Mass Deception," "The principle of individuality was always full of contradiction . . . the individual who supported society, bore its disfiguring mark; seemingly free, he was actually the product of its economic and social apparatus . . . The only reason why the culture industry can deal so successfully with individuality is that the latter has always reproduced the fragility of society" (T.W. Adorno and M. Horkheimer, *Dialectic of Enlightenment*, p. 155.).

33 T.W. Adorno, "Freudian Theory and the Pattern of Fascist Propaganda," p. 119.

34 "The Psychological Technique of Martin Luther Thomas's Radio Addresses," p. 27.

35 Ibid., n.

36 The gendered term is apt: for all his attention to the libidinal substratum of fascist propaganda, Adorno hardly ever seems to regard gender divisions as salient: fascism is men's work.

37 "Freudian Theory and the Pattern of Fascist Propaganda," p. 122.

38 "Anti-Semitism and Fascist Propaganda," this volume, p. 167.
39 See ibid., p. 170.
40 "The Psychological Technique of Martin Luther Thomas's Radio Addresses," p. 72.
41 "Anti-Semitism and Fascist Propaganda," this volume, p. 170.
42 T.W. Adorno and M. Horkheimer, *Dialectic of Enlightenment*, p. 185.
43 "Anti-Semitism and Fascist propaganda," this volume, p. 167.
44 Ibid., p. 168.
45 "The Psychological Technique of Martin Luther Thomas's Radio Addresses," pp. 14, 21, 23.
46 "Anti-Semitism and Fascist Propaganda," this volume, p. 168.
47 "The Psychological Technique of Martin Luther Thomas's Radio Addresses," p. 32.
48 Ibid., p. 52.
49 Ibid., p. 54.
50 Ibid.
51 "The Stars Down to Earth," this volume, p. 57.
52 Ibid., p. 65.
53 Ibid.
54 Ibid.
55 Ibid., p. 67 (emphasis throughout in the original).
56 Ibid., p. 68.
57 Ibid., p. 74.
58 Ibid., p. 71.
59 "The Psychological Technique of Martin Luther Thomas's Radio Addresses," p. 39.
60 "The Stars Down to Earth," this volume, pp. 104–5.
61 Ibid., p. 104.
62 Ibid., p. 102.
63 Ibid., p. 53.
64 "The Psychological Technique of Martin Luther Thomas's Radio Addresses," p. 40.
65 "Anti-Semitism and Fascist Propaganda," this volume, p. 66.
66 "The Psychological Technique of Martin Luther Thomas's Radio Addresses," p. 88.
67 Ibid., p. 88. See also "Anti-Semitism and Fascist Propaganda," this volume p. 167. Adorno's conception of folk-culture contains an implicit critique of theories of the unsullied and archetypal "authenticity" of an inherently resistant popular culture, Bakhtin-derived versions of which are still current in cultural studies.
68 "The Psychological Technique of Martin Luther Thomas's Radio Addresses," p. 89.
69 Ibid., p. 90.
70 S. Jhally, "Advertising as Religion: the Dialectic of Technology and Magic," in I. Angus and S. Jhally (eds), *Cultural Politics in Contemporary America*. New York: Routledge, 1989, p. 217.
71 T.W. Adorno, "The Psychological Technique of Martin Luther Thomas's Radio Addresses," p. 22. A little earlier (p. 15), Adorno observes that agitators using the "Lone Wolf" device may be surrounded by bodyguards

while claiming to stand alone against the enemy. He notes that "they do not expect it to be taken quite seriously, and it probably never is."

72 "Introduction" to T.W. Adorno, *The Culture Industry* (ed. J.M. Bernstein). London: Routledge, 1991, pp. 10–4. Perhaps because Bernstein's account is based wholly on "Stars," which makes little direct reference to jokes, he does not register the role that jokiness or humour might play in the syndrome.

73 "The Stars Down to Earth," this volume, p. 36.

74 Ibid., p. 36.

75 Ibid.

76 "Theses Against Occultism," this volume, p. 129.

77 Ibid., p. 129.

78 Ibid., p. 130.

79 "Anti-Semitism and Fascist Propaganda," this volume, p. 165.

80 "The Psychological Technique of Martin Luther Thomas's Radio Addresses," p. 65.

81 Ibid., p. 14.

82 Ibid., p. 18.

83 Ibid., p. 39.

84 Ibid., p. 81.

85 "Anti-Semitism and Fascist Propaganda," this volume p. 166.

86 "The Psychological Technique of Martin Luther Thomas's Radio Addresses," p. 18.

87 "The Stars Down to Earth," this volume, p. 39.

88 Ibid., p. 45.

89 Ibid., p. 115.

90 For a brief discussion see M. Jay, *Adorno*. London: Fontana, 1984, ch. 4. For the editor's view see S. Crook, *Modernist Radicalism and its Aftermath*, London: Routledge, 1991, pp. 89–105.

91 "The Stars Down to Earth," this volume, p. 38.

92 "The Psychological Technique of Martin Luther Thomas's Radio Addresses," p. 13.

93 "The Stars Down to Earth," this volume, p. 39.

94 See the discussion in M. Jay, *The Dialectical Imagination*, pp. 222–3.

95 See, for example, the first section of J.P. Tompkins (ed.), *Reader Response Criticism*. Baltimore: Johns Hopkins University Press, 1980.

96 M. Billig, *Arguing and Thinking: a Rhetorical Approach to Social Psychology*. Cambridge: Cambridge University Press, 1987, pp. 177–8.

97 M. Billig, *Ideology and Opinions*. London: Sage, 1991, p. 126.

98 See W. Reich, *The Mass Psychology of Fascism*. Harmondsworth: Penguin, 1970. H. Marcuse, *Eros and Civilization: A Philosophical Enquiry into Freud*. Boston: Beacon Press, 1955.

99 See for example "The Psychological Technique of Martin Luther Thomas's Radio Addresses," pp. 14, 18, 51.

100 G. Allport, *The Meaning of Prejudice*. Reading, Mass.: Addison–Wesley, 1954.

101 See C. Bagley *et al.*, *Personality, Self-Esteem and Prejudice*. Farnborough: Saxon House, 1979. C. Bagley and G. Verma, *Racial Prejudice, the Individual and Society*. Farnborough: Saxon House, 1979.

102 B. Altemeyer, *Enemies of Freedom*. San Francisco: Jossey-Bass, 1988.
103 A comparison of "Frankfurt School" concerns with those of the interactionist tradition is offered by N.K. Denzin, *Symbolic Interactionism and Cultural Studies*. Oxford: Blackwell, 1992, pp. 112–14. Sadly, Denzin simply re-draws the usual caricature. However, there is no reason in principle why accounts of the interactional production of "self" could not articulate a model of the systematic production of individuals with high dependency-needs. In the area of what is usually termed "postmodernist" culture theory, Adorno has been compared with both Derrida and Foucault (for a brief review see M. Jay, "Adorno in America" in his *Permanent Exiles*. New York: Columbia University Press, 1986, pp. 133–6. Some parallels between Adorno and Baudrillard are noted below.
104 M. Billig, *Fascists: a Social Psychological View of the National Front*. London: Harcourt, Brace Jovanovich, 1978, p. 41.
105 Z. Bauman, *Modernity and the Holocaust*. Cambridge: Polity Press, 1989, ch. 3.
106 Ibid., chs. 4, 6.
107 Ibid., p. 153.
108 M. Billig, *Fascists*, p. 38.
109 D. Harris, *From Class Struggle to the Politics of Pleasure*. London: Routledge, 1992, p. 14.
110 I. Angus and S. Jhally (eds), *Cultural Politics in Contemporary America*.
111 J. McGuigan, *Cultural Populism*. London: Routledge, 1992, p. 244.
112 I. Angus and S. Jhally, "Introduction" to *Cultural Politics in Contemporary America*, pp. 6, 13.
113 J. McGuigan, *Cultural Populism*, p. 48.
114 Of course, the populists who make the most fuss about popular pleasures are the last people to take them at face value: pleasures are heavily glossed as "really" about resistance, liberation etc. McGuigan gives a useful and succinct critique of Fiske's particularly florid populism in *Cultural Populism*, pp. 70–5.
115 J.M. Bernstein, "Introduction" to T.W. Adorno, *The Culture Industry*, p. 20.
116 For example, see A. Tomlinson, "Introduction" in his (ed.) *Consumption, Identity and Style*. London: Routledge, 1990, p. 6.
117 F. Jameson, *Late Marxism: Adorno or the Persistence of the Dialectic*. London: Verso, 1990, p. 252.
118 J.M. Bernstein, "Introduction" to T.W. Adorno, *The Culture Industry*, pp. 20–1.
119 T.W. Adorno, "The Schematism of Mass Culture," ibid., p. 71.
120 I. Hassan, "The Culture of Postmodernism," *Theory, Culture and Society* 2, 1985, pp. 119–32.
121 See M. Jay, *The Dialectical Imagination*, p. 247.
122 J. Baudrillard, "Simulacra and Simulations," in his *Selected Writings*. Cambridge: Polity Press, 1988, p. 182.

1

THE STARS DOWN TO EARTH:
THE *LOS ANGELES TIMES*
ASTROLOGY COLUMN

INTRODUCTION

The group of studies to which the content analysis of the *Los Angeles Times* astrology column belongs, sets as its aim the investigation of the nature and motivations of some large-scale social phenomena involving irrational elements in a peculiar way – fused with what may be dubbed pseudo-rationality. Various mass movements spread all over the world in which people seem to act against their own rational interests of self-preservation and the "pursuit of happiness" have been evident now for a considerable length of time. It would be a mistake, however, to call such mass phenomena entirely "irrational," to regard them as completely disconnected from individual and collective ego aims. In fact, most of them are based on an exaggeration and distortion of such ego aims rather than on their neglect. They function as though rationality of the self-maintaining body politic had grown malignant and therewith threatened to destroy the organism. This malignancy, however, can be demonstrated only after the autopsy. Often enough the consequence of apparently rational considerations leads to ultimately fatal events – the most recent example being Hitler's shrewd and temporarily highly successful policy of national expansion which by its own logic inexorably led to his doom and world catastrophe. In fact, even when whole nations assume the role of profiteers of *Realpolitik*, this rationality is only partial and dubious. While the calculations of self-interest are pushed to extremes, the view of the totality of factors, and in particular, of the effects of such a policy upon the whole seems to be strangely curtailed. Overly shrewd concentration on self-interest results in a crippling of the capacity to look beyond the limits of self-interest and this finally works against itself. Irrationality is not necessarily a force operating outside the range of rationality: it may result from the processes of rational self preservation "run amuck."

34

It is the pattern of interacting rational and irrational forces in modern mass movements upon which our studies hope to throw some light. The danger is by no means, as some theories such as Brickner's *Is Germany Incurable?*[1] would like to have it, a specific German illness, the collective paranoia of one particular nation, but seems to spring from more universal social and cultural conditions. One of the most important contributions psychiatry and psychoanalytically-oriented sociology can make in this respect is to reveal certain mechanisms which cannot be grasped adequately either in terms of being sensible or in terms of delusions. Their investigation points to a definite basis in certain subjective dispositions though they certainly cannot be explained altogether psychologically. Psychotic character structure may sometimes though by no means always, be involved. In view of the presupposition of psychological "susceptibility" it may be assumed that they do not manifest themselves only in the sphere of politics that is at least on the surface realistic, but can be studied in other social areas as well, or even better, although the reality factor is rarely absent even from fads which somehow pride themselves on their own irrationality. Such an approach might be less hampered by rationalizations which in the field of politics are hard to discount. It also might violate fewer taboos and deep-rooted canons of behavior. Above all, it should be possible to analyze the inner structure of such movements on a small test-tube scale, as it were, and at a time when they do not yet manifest themselves so directly and threateningly that there is no time left for objective and detached research. The danger of *ex post facto* theories might thus be partially avoided.

It is in this spirit that we take up the study of astrology, not because we overrate its importance as a social phenomenon *per se*, nefarious though it is in various respects. Accordingly, the specific nature of our study is not a direct psychoanalysis of the occult, of the type initiated by Freud's famous essay "The Uncanny"[2] and followed up by numerous scientific ventures, now collected by Dr. Devereux in *Psychoanalysis and the Occult*.[3] We do not want to examine occult experiences or individual superstitious beliefs of any kind as expressions of the unconscious. In fact, the occult as such plays only a marginal role in systems such as organized astrology. Its sphere has little enough in common with that of the spiritualist who sees or hears ghosts or with telepathy. In analogy with the sociological differentiation of primary or secondary groups,[4] we may define our area of interest as one of "secondary superstition." By this we mean that the individual's own primary experience of the occult, whatever its psychological meaning and roots or its validity, rarely, if ever, enter the social phenomenon to which our studies are devoted. Here, the occult appears rather institutionalized, objectified and, to a large extent, socialized. Just as in secondary communities, people no longer "live together" and know each other directly, but are related to each other through intermediary objectified social processes (e.g., exchange of commodities), so people responding to the stimuli we are here investigating seem in a way "alien" to the experience on which they claim their decisions are based. They participate in them largely through the mediation of magazines and newspapers, the personal advice of professional astrologers being too expensive, and frequently accept such information as reliable sources of advice rather than pretend to have any personal basis for their belief. The type of people we are concerned with take astrology for granted, much like psychiatry, symphony concerts or political parties; they accept it because it *exists*, without much reflection, provided only that their own psychological demands somehow correspond to the offer. They are hardly interested in the justification of the system. In the newspaper column to which this monograph is mainly devoted the mechanics of the astrological system are never divulged and the readers are presented only with the alleged results of astrological reasoning in which the reader does not actively participate.

This alienation from experience, a certain abstractness enveloping the whole realm of the commercialized occult may well be concomitant with a substratum of disbelief and skepticism, the suspicion of phoniness so deeply associated with modern big time irrationality. This, of course, has historical reasons. The modern occultist movements, including astrology, are more or less artificial rehashes of old and by-gone superstitions, susceptibility for which is kept awake by certain social and psychological conditions while the resuscitated creeds remain basically discordant with today's universal state of enlightenment. The absence of ultimate "seriousness" which, incidentally, makes such phenomena by no means less serious with regard to their social implications – is as significant of our time as the emergence of secondary occultism *per se*.

It may be objected that organized fortune telling has for time immemorial had the character of "secondary superstition." It has been separated for thousands of years from whatever could be called primary experience through a division of labor that admitted only priests into the esoteric mystery and therefore always carried within itself the element of phoniness expressed in the old Latin adage that an augur laughs when he sees another. As always with arguments intended to discredit interest in the specific modernity of phenomena by stressing that there is nothing new under the sun, this objection is both true and false. It is true in as much as the institutionalization of superstition is by no means novel; it is false in so far as this institutionalization has reached, by means of mass production, a quantity which is likely to result in a new quality of attitudes and behavior and in that the gap between the systems of superstition and the general state of mind has been widened tremendously. We may here refer only to the aforementioned detachment of large groups of believers from the "working" of superstition, and to their interest in net results rather than in supposedly supranatural powers. They don't even see the sorcerers at work any more nor are they allowed to listen to their abracadabra. They simply "get the dope." In addition, it should be stressed that in former periods, superstition was an attempt, however awkward, to cope with problems for which no better or more rational means were available at least so far as the masses are concerned. The sharp division between alchemy and chemistry, between astrology and astronomy is a comparatively late achievement. Today, however, the incompatibility of the progress of natural sciences, such as astro-physics, with a belief in astrology is blatant. Those who combine both are forced to an intellectual retrogression which formerly was hardly required. In a world in which, through popular scientific literature and particularly science fiction, every schoolboy knows of the billions of galaxies, the cosmic insignificance of the earth and the mechanical laws governing the movements of stellar systems, the geocentric and anthropocentric view concomitant with astrology is utterly anachronistic. We thus may assume that only very strong instinctual demands make it possible for people still – or anew – to accept astrology. Under present conditions, the astrological system *can* function only as "secondary superstition," largely exempt from the individual's own critical control and offered authoritatively.

It is necessary to stress this character of "secondary superstition" since it provides the key for one of the strangest elements in the material we are investigating. This is just its pseudo-rationality, the very same traits that play such a conspicuous role in totalitarian social movements, its calculative though spurious adaptation to realistic needs. Again, this may have been germane to fortune telling since time immemorial. People always wanted to learn from occult signs what to expect and do; in fact, superstition is largely a residue of animistic magical practices by which ancient humanity tried to influence or control the course of events. But the sobriety, nay the overrealism, of our material at the expense of anything remotely reminiscent of the supranatural seems to be one of its most paradoxical and challenging features. Overrealism in itself may be, in some directions, irrational, in the sense of that overdeveloped and self-destructive shrewdness of self interest, pointed out before. In addition it will be proved during the course of our study that astrological irrationality has largely been reduced to a purely formal characteristic: abstract authority.

Our interest in secondary superstition naturally entails a lesser concentration on the psychological explanations of individual occult leanings than in the total personality set-up of those who are susceptible to these rather ubiquitous stimuli. In order to approach the problem, psychiatric as well as socio-psychological categories will have to be utilized. In view of the interweaving of rational and irrational elements, we are mainly interested in the direct or indirect "messages" conveyed by the material to its consumers: such messages combine irrationality (in as much as they aim at blind acceptance and presuppose unconscious anger in the consumers) and rationality (in as much as they deal with more or less practical everyday problems for which they pretend to offer the most helpful answer). Very often it seems as though astrology were only an authoritarian cloak while the matter itself is strongly reminiscent of a mental health column written for the trade in limited self-awareness and paternal support. The column attempts to satisfy the longings of people who are thoroughly convinced that others (or some unknown agency) ought to know more about themselves and what they should do than they can decide for themselves. It is this "mundane" aspect of astrology which particularly invites social and psychological interpretation. In fact, many of the messages are of a directly social or psychological nature. However, they rarely if ever adequately express social or psychological reality, but manipulate the readers' ideas of such matters in a definite direction. Therefore, they must not be taken at face value, but subjected to some deeper probing.

This study is in the nature of content analysis. About three months of the daily column "Astrological Forecasts" by Carroll Righter in the *Los Angeles Times*. November 1952–February 1953, are interpreted. As a corollary, some observations on a number of astrological magazines are presented. We want to give a picture of the specific stimuli operating on followers of astrology whom we hypothetically regard as representative of the whole group of those who go for 'secondary occultism' and of the presumptive effect of these stimuli. We assume that such publications mold some ways of their readers' thinking; yet they pretend to adjust themselves to the readers' needs, wants, wishes and demands in order to "sell." We regard this content analysis as an inroad to the study of the mentality of larger groups of a similar frame of mind.

There are various reasons for choosing this material. Limitations of research facilities prevented real field work and forced us to concentrate on printed material rather than on primary reactions. Such material seemed to be most copious in astrology and was easily accessible. Also astrology probably has the largest following among the various occultist schools in the population. It is certainly not one of the extreme occultist trades, but puts up a facade of pseudo-rationality which makes it easier to embrace than, for example, spiritualism. No wraiths appear, and the forecasts pretend to be derived from astronomic facts. Thus astrology might not bring out so clearly psychotic mechanisms as those fashions indulged in by the real lunatic fringe of superstition. This may hamper our study as far as understanding of the deeper unconscious layers of neo-occultism is concerned. This potential disadvantage, however, is compensated by the fact that astrology has caught on in such large sections of the population that the findings in as much as they partly are confined to the ego level and to social determinants, may be generalized with greater confidence. Moreover, it is just "pseudo-rationality," the twilight zone between reason and unconscious urges, in which we are specifically interested from the viewpoint of social psychology.

For the time being our study has to limit itself to the qualitative. It represents an attempt to understand what astrological publications mean in terms of reader reactions, on an overt level as well as on a deeper one. While this analysis is guided by psychoanalytic concepts, it should be pointed out from the very beginning that our approach as far as it largely involves social attitudes and actions must largely consider conscious or semiconscious phases. It would be inappropriate to think exclusively in terms of the unconscious where *the stimuli themselves* are consciously calculated and institutionalized to such an extent that their power of directly reaching the unconscious should not be regarded as absolute and where overt issues of self-interest continuously enter the picture. Frequently, surface aims are fused with vicarious gratifications of the unconscious.

In fact, the concept of the unconscious cannot be posited dogmatically in any study concerning the border area of psychological determinants and social attitudes. In the whole field of mass communications, the "hidden meaning" is not truly unconscious at all, but represents a layer which is neither quite admitted nor quite repressed – the sphere of innuendo, the winking of an eye and "you know what I mean." Frequently one encounters a kind of "mimicking" of the unconscious in the maintenance of certain taboos which, however, are not fully endorsed. No light has so far been thrown on this somewhat obscure psychological zone, and our study should among other things contribute to its understanding. It goes without saying that the ultimate basis of this zone has to be sought in the truly unconscious, but it might be a dangerous fallacy to regard the psychological twilight of numerous mass reactions as straightforward manifestations of the instincts.

So far as effectiveness upon actual reader mentality is concerned, our results must by necessity be regarded as tentative. They provide us with formulations, the validity of which can and should only be established by reader research. We may expect that the authors of our material know what they are doing and to whom they are talking, though they themselves may start from hunches or stereotyped assumptions concerning their readers which facts would not bear out. Moreover, there is little doubt that in any modern mass communications the idea is artificially fostered that one has to cater to the tastes of some group as a means to mold the communication material in a way fitting the mentality of those responsible for the production or their designs. Shifting responsibility from the manipulators to the manipulated is a widespread ideological pattern. We must therefore be cautious not to treat our material dogmatically as a mirrored reflection of the reader's mind.

Conversely, we do not try to make inferences through our analysis about the mentality of those responsible for the publications to be examined, particularly the authors. We do not think that such a study would lead us very far. Even in the sphere of art, the idea of projection has been largely overrated. Although the author's motivations certainly enter the artifact, they are by no means so all-determining as is often assumed. As soon as an artist has set himself his problem, it obtains some kind of impact of its own, and in most cases he has to follow the objective requirements of his product much more than his own urges of expression when he translates his primary conception into artistic reality. To be sure, these objective requirements do not play a decisive role in mass media which stress consumer effect far beyond any artistic or intellectual problem. However, the total set-up here tends to limit the chances of projection utterly. Those who produce the material follow innumerable requirements, rules of thumb, set patterns and mechanisms of controls which by necessity reduce to a minimum the range of any kind of self-expression.

Certainly the author's motivations are but one source while the set patterns to which they have to stick seem far more important. While it would be very hard to trace back a production like the *Los Angeles Times* column to any single source in particular, it is integrated in such a way that the material speaks a kind of language of its own which can be read and understood even if we do not know much about the processes which led to the formulation of the language and infused it with meaning. It ought to be stressed that understanding of such a language cannot confine itself to its single morphemes, but always has to remain conscious of the total pattern in which these morphemes are more or less mechanically interwoven. Some particular devices cropping up in our material such as for example frequent reference to the family background of a person born on a certain day may appear completely trivial and harmless if seen in isolation. In the functional unity of the whole, however, they may obtain a significance far beyond the harmless and comforting idea which is indicated at first sight.

BASIC SITUATION OF THE COLUMN

The column "Astrological Forecasts" by Carroll Righter appears in the *Los Angeles Times*, a conservative newspaper leaning far to the right wing of the Republican Party. Mr. Righter is well-known in movie circles and supposed to be the private astrological counselor to one of the most famous film "stars." When he took up his work, he obtained considerable publicity also in television. However, his column does not indicate any particular tinge of Hollywood sensationalism or Southern California faddism. The whole outlook of the column is "moderate." There are only isolated manifestations of obvious superstition or overt irrationalities. Irrationality is rather kept in the background, defining the basis of the whole approach: it is treated as a matter of course that the various prognoses and the corresponding advice are derived from the stars. Astrological niceties and astrological lingo except for the popular twelve signs of the zodiac are absent. The more sinister aspects of astrology such as emphasis on catastrophes and threatening doom hardly make themselves felt. Everything sounds respectable, sedate and sensible and astrology as such is treated as something established and socially recognized, an uncontroversial element of our culture, as though it were somewhat bashful of its own shadiness. Hardly ever does the practical advice tendered to the reader transgress the limits of what one finds in any column dealing with human relations and popular psychology. The only difference is that the writer leans on his distinctly magical and irrational authority which seems to be strangely out of proportion with the common-sense content of what he has to offer. This discrepancy cannot be regarded as accidental. The common-sense advice itself contains, as will be shown later, many spurious "pseudo-rational" elements, calling for some authoritarian backing to be effective. At the same time, the reluctance of the readers to be "sensible" in just the way the column advocates it, may make for a response which can only be overcome by conjuring up the image of some absolute power. This authoritarian element, incidentally, is also present in the popular psychological columns of which the column is reminiscent in so many respects: their authority is wielded by the expert rather than by the "Magus" while the latter also feels compelled to speak as an expert.

Yet, the implicit irrationality of the column's claim to be inspired by the stars cannot be dismissed in as much as it sets the stage for its effect and fulfils a highly significant function in dealing with the anxieties and difficulties of those at whom the column is directed. Astrology, although it sometimes pretends to be chummy with theology, is basically different from religion. The irrationality of the source is not only kept remote, but is also treated as impersonal and thing-like: there is an underlying philosophy of what might be called naturalist supranaturalism. This "depersonalized" merciless aspect of the supposedly transcendent source has much to do with the latent threat spelled by astrology. The source remains entirely abstract, unapproachable and anonymous. This reflects the type of irrationality in which the total order of our life presents itself to most individuals: opaqueness and inscrutability. Naive persons fail to look through the complexities of a highly organized and institutionalized society, but even the sophisticated ones cannot understand it in plain terms of consistency and reason, but are faced with antagonism and absurdities, the most blatant of which is the threat brought to mankind by the very same technology which was furthered in order to make life easier. Who wants to survive under present conditions is tempted to "accept" such absurdities, like the verdict of the stars, rather than to penetrate them by thinking which means discomfort in many directions. In this respect, astrology is truly in harmony with a ubiquitous trend. In as much as the social system is the "fate" of most individuals independent of their will and interest, it is projected upon the stars in order thus to obtain a higher degree of dignity and justification in which the individuals hope to participate themselves. At the same time, the idea that the stars, if one only reads them correctly, offer some advice mitigates the very same fear of the inexorability of social processes the stargazer himself creates. This phase of astrology's own ambivalence is exploited by the "rational" side of the column. The aid and comfort given by the merciless stars is tantamount to the idea that only he who behaves rationally, i.e., achieves complete control over his inner and outer life, has any chance of doing justice to the irrational contradictory requirements of the existent by adjustment. Thus, the discrepancy between the rational and the irrational aspects of the column is expressive

42

of a tension inherent in social reality itself. "To be rational" means not questioning irrational conditions, but to make the best of them from the viewpoint of one's private interests. A truly unconscious aspect, primitive and possibly decisive, but never allowed to come to the fore in the column, should at least be suggested. Indulgence in astrology may provide those who fall for it with a substitute for sexual pleasure of a passive nature. It means primarily submission to unbridled strength of the absolute power. However, this strength and power ultimately derived from the father image has become completely depersonalized in astrology. Communion with the stars is an almost unrecognizable and therefore tolerable substitute of the forbidden relation with an omnipotent father figure. People are allowed to enjoy communion with absolute strength in as much as it is considered no longer human. It seems likely that the fantasies about world destruction and ultimate doom appearing in more extremist astrological publications than the *Los Angeles Times* column are connected with this ultimately sexual content in as much as they are the last vestige of the individual expression of guilt feelings grown as unrecognizable as their libidinal source. Apart from this zone, the stars mean sex without threat. They are depicted as omnipotent, but they are very far away even farther than the narcissistic leader figures described in Freud's "Group Psychology and the Analysis of the Ego."[5]

THE COLUMN AND THE ASTROLOGICAL MAGAZINES

At this point, it may be pertinent to characterize briefly the difference between the column and astrological magazines such as *Forecast, Astrology Guide, American Astrology, World Astrology, True Astrology, Everyday Astrology* and other publications of the "pulp" type. While no systematic study of this material could so far be undertaken, it has been perused to a sufficient degree to allow a comparison with the *Los Angeles Times* column which contributes toward an understanding of the latter's proper setting. There are numerous shades in the magazine material ranging from very harmless, though utterly primitive, publications such as *World Astrology* to wilder ones such as *True Astrology* or *Everyday Astrology* to paranoid ones such as *American Astrology*. No degree of secondary occultism has been forgotten. Our observations, however, seem valid for all these magazines on the basis of a cursory comparison.

It goes without saying that such magazines directed at a nucleus of astrological followers rather than at the public at large contain more "technical" astrological material and try to impress the readers both with "esoteric" knowledge and with "scientific" elaborateness. Terms such as "house," "square," "opposition," etc., occur all the time. Astrology is not taken for granted, but attempts with some violence to defend its "status." Thus, the issue from which our examples are chosen, contains a polemic against some doctor of science who criticized astrology as a superstition and compared it with fortune telling from the entrails of animals or from the flight of birds.[6] The magazines seem to be particularly sensitive about any such comparison. The doctor's charges are denied through the somewhat tautological assertion that astrology never busies itself with entrails or birds. It pretends to a higher level of scientificness than the supposedly more primitive forms of esoteric wisdom without, however, entering into the argument itself: the lack of a transparent interconnection between astronomical observations and inferences pertaining to the fate of individuals or nations.

The only substantial difference more sophisticated astrologers can point out between themselves and the tribe of crystal-gazers is their aversion to unqualified prophecies – an attitude presumably due to caution. They reiterate continuously that they are not determinists. Here they fall in line with the pattern of modern mass culture which protests the more fanatically about the tenets of individualism and the freedom of the will, the more actual freedom of action vanishes. Astrology attempts to get away from crude and unpopular fatalism by establishing outward forces operating on the individual's decision, including the individual's own character, but leaves the ultimate choice to him. This has significant socio-psychological implications. Astrology undertakes the constant encouragement of people to take decisions, no matter how inconsequential they may be. It is practically directed towards action in spite of all the lofty talk about cosmic secrets and profound meditation. Thus, the very gesture of astrology, its basic presumption that everyone has to make up his mind at every moment falls in line with what will later come out with respect to the specific content of astrological counseling: its leaning towards extroversion. Moreover, the idea that the freedom of the individual amounts to nothing more than making the best of what a given constellation of stars permits implies the very same idea of adjustment the affinity to which has been pointed out previously as one of the traits of astrology. According to this concept, freedom consists of the individual's taking upon himself voluntarily what is inevitable anyway. The empty shell of liberty is solicitously kept intact. If the individual acts according to given conjunctions, everything will go right, if he does not, everything will go wrong. Sometimes it is quite frankly stated that the individual should adjust himself to certain constellations.

One might say that there is in astrology an implicit metaphysics of adjustment behind the concretistic advice of adjustment in everyday life. Thus the philosophy expressed by the speculations of the magazines provides us actually with some background for the understanding of the down-to-earth statements of the *Los Angeles Times* column.

It may be reiterated that the climate of semi-erudition is the fertile breeding-ground for astrology because here primary naivete, the unreflecting acceptance of the existent has been lost whereas at the same time neither the power of thinking nor positive knowledge has been developed sufficiently. The semi-erudite vaguely wants to understand and is also driven by the narcissistic wish to prove superior to the plain people but he is not in a position to carry through complicated and detached intellectual operations. To him, astrology, just as other irrational creeds like racism, provides a short-cut by bringing the complex to a handy formula and offering at the same time the pleasant gratification that he who feels to be excluded from educational privileges nevertheless belongs to the minority of those who are "in the know." In accordance with this kind of gratification, the whole atmosphere is much more grandiloquent and boastful of the wisdom of the initiated and bombastic predictions go to much greater extremes than the *Times* column. As was to be expected, there are frequent sinister hints such as those of the beginning of the new era heralding a major world catastrophe and implying a war between the United States and Russia in 1953 without, however, committing itself definitely on this score.

Nevertheless, the caution prevailing in the *Los Angeles Times* column is also shown to a certain extent even in such scurrilous publications. Thus it is stated in one article with amazing frankness that there is no uniformity about the basic interpretation of heavenly signs among astrologists, probably an attempt to ward off any attacks based on the inconsistencies between various astrological forecasts. As a matter of fact, there are flagrant contradictions to be found among various articles in a single issue. The publisher and editor in one case wrote a lead article tuned to the impending doom idea and the prediction of a terrible battle in which the American 'majority' – a notion which might have a racist slant while sounding democratic – is going to win. This, however, is followed immediately by another article which heralds the new year as one of bliss promising that it will relieve innumerable people of worries and pressures. Obviously an attempt is being made to cater to various layers of demands in the readers, to those more deep-lying ones where the spectacle of the twilight of the gods is hoped for as well as to the level where one wants to be reassured about a raise in one's salary.

A kind of middle way between realism and paranoid fantasies is sought in the political harangues of the magazine. Several times, though always somewhat vaguely, the magazines accuse disruptive minorities, leaving it open who is meant. Some of the imagery reminds one of that used by fascist anti-Semitic agitators of the pseudo-religious brand. Thus reference is made to the apocalyptic battle of Armageddon which played a large role in the speeches of a Los Angeles "radio priest" who created quite a stir during the 1930s. However, it is possible that such biblical imagery is used independently of the vernacular of political agitators and draws its strength from the tradition of revivalism. Nevertheless the heavy employment of the "impending doom" device is hardly accidental. It encourages the addressee's destructive urges and feeds on their discomfort in civilization, while at the same time stirring up a bellicose mood.

Altogether, however, the American cultural climate seems to demand at least a veneer of common sense and realism. This leads to the truly unexpected features of the magazines which happen to be just the opposite of the eccentricities just referred to. There seems to be more implied than merely American common sense and realism. In the magazines, one finds entirely different zones, carefully kept apart from each other. On the one hand, there are general astrological speculations involving conjunctions, oppositions, houses, etc. They are being applied to mankind as a whole, or at least to the American nation as such. On the other hand, there are detailed predictions of what will happen on each day to any person born under a specific sign of the zodiac. The main difference between the *Los Angeles Times* column and the astrological magazines is that the column carries only the latter predictions and the horoscopes of children born on a particular day and omits the "speculative" and world-historical material contained in the magazines. However, if one compares predictions in the column and in the magazines, there is, apart from individual difference of style and preferences of the writers, a striking similarity.[7]

Winter Issue (1953) of Forecast
Daily Advice for Virgo, p. 59

MONDAY 16 FEBRUARY Don't attempt to tell someone what you think of them or to criticize unfavorably. Be wise and know that silence is the best part of valor today. Put your energies into some needed work or a job that has been awaiting your attention.

TUESDAY 17 FEBRUARY There seems to be considerable tension

around you; see that you do not add fuel to the fire. Relax; read a good book or do something that will occupy your mind and hands in a constructive manner. Retire early.

WEDNESDAY 18 FEBRUARY All constructive effort, whether of a personal or business nature, should bring good results and benefit to you. Make dates, appointments or interviews.

THURSDAY 19 FEBRUARY Get started early with your personal plans; travel, write, seek aid or instruction, see lawyers, advisors or instructors, doctors, nurses, agents, or repairmen, friends or teachers.

FRIDAY 20 FEBRUARY Don't attempt to do the impossible; finish the routine work or job and wait for a better time to start new or important projects. Enjoy some special friendship or a show in the evening.

SATURDAY 21 FEBRUARY The day can be slightly difficult unless you are willing to cooperate and adapt to present conditions. Don't be too critical; display a sense of humor.

SUNDAY 22 FEBRUARY Whatever it is that you want to do today, if it helps another in any way, do it. Work or pleasure shared will be pleasant and beneficial in many respects.

MONDAY 23 FEBRUARY You must exercise caution with all associates, and keep out of disputes or arguments which could lower you in the estimation of some important people.

TUESDAY 24 FEBRUARY This is a good time to take stock of your assets and see where you can make some advantageous changes or investments. See officials, make agreements or appointments, phone, visit or write.

WEDNESDAY 25 FEBRUARY If you expect progress in anything today, you must put forth some extra effort and work. See that all jobs, tasks of a home nature and related correspondence is brought up to date.

THURSDAY 26 FEBRUARY Early hours of the day give the best chance for attending to any important matters or the starting of anything new. Be a little cautious in dealing with legal matters, foreign correspondence and financial affairs later.

FRIDAY 27 FEBRUARY Don't be too disturbed by news or commotions around you. Confine your efforts to the worthwhile activities in connection with your home or place of business. Keep calm, relaxed and ready to cooperate with all people.

SATURDAY 28 FEBRUARY Take it easy, and don't let your temper or impulses rule your better judgment. It pays to ignore the things or statements you don't like, and take a constructive viewpoint of things.

Carroll Righter's "Astrological Forecast"
Column for Saturday, 31 January 1953.

ARIES: Make your appearance more charming early. Then, contact co-workers and make plans for a more efficient and harmonious arrangement of future routine chores.

TAURUS: Attend to essential home duties early; then venture forth and make yourself more charming by means of beauty treatments, haircuts, dieting. In P.M. have fun; be happy.

GEMINI: Contact all and complete business and correspondence early. Later, pitch in and make home, family and property conditions more satisfactory through cooperative measures.

CANCER: Find out early just where you stand financially and then go out and attend to necessary red tape. Confer with associates who understand your urges; seek their help.

LEO: Decide early what you want, and then study your income and expenses; then, devise new imaginative ways to increase your revenue to take care of new expenses; seek abundance.

VIRGO: Consult a confidante early and plan for attainment of mutual desires; make sure you know your specific part in the arrangement. See all who can help your advance.

LIBRA: A good friend points the way to your desires: in appreciation, do as suggested; quietly channeling your efforts without fanfare, for, in this case, secrecy is best.

SCORPIO: Find out early exactly what an important person expects from you; then contact a good friend who can help you; be readily cooperative and success will follow.

SAGITTARIUS: Early in the A.M. a prophetic hunch requires that you contact a powerful person who is able to make your inspiration a success. Be exact all through the day.

CAPRICORN: Make a working plan early for increasing joint revenue. Then, get in touch with new acquaintances who can use their expert knowledge to make the project a success.

AQUARIUS: Placate your opponent and huddle with a partner early in the A.M. Then make a specific outline of an effective working arrangement and all concerned are delighted.

PISCES: Complete all your duties at breakfast time and leave the rest of the day free to have fun with all associates. Take no chances; discuss all points of interest.

The striking feature which the personal predictions in the two kinds of publications have in common is their "practicability" and the almost complete absence of any reference to the major and mostly solemn speculations about the fate of mankind at large. It is as though the sphere of the individual were completely severed from that of the "world" or the cosmos. The slogan "business as usual" is accepted as a kind of metaphysical maxim.

In view of the obvious absurdity of tendering petty advice to people who at the same time are fed with glowing images of all-embracing conflicts, this dichotomy calls for an interpretation. Mention should be made of the theory of Ernst Simmel that delusions such as totalitarian anti-Semitism are within the individual "isolated" and at the same time collectivized, thus preventing the individual from actually becoming psychotic.[8] This structure is reflected by the dichotomy here under discussion. It is as though astrology has to provide gratifications to aggressive urges on the level of the imaginary, but is not allowed to interfere too obviously with the "normal' functioning of the individual in reality. Rather than impairing the individual's reality testing it at least superficially tries to strengthen his capacity.

In this respect, some similarity to the function of the dream suggests itself. As is generally known since Freud, the dream is the protector of sleep by fulfilling conscious and unconscious wishes, which waking life is incapable of gratifying, by hallucinatory imagery. The dream content has often been likened in its function to psychotic delusions. It is as though the ego protected itself from the onslaught of instinctual material by its translation into dreams. This is relatively innocuous because it is generally confined to the ideational sphere. Only in isolated cases, such as sleep walking, does it gain control of the motoric apparatus. Thus it may be said that dreams not only protect sleep, but also the waking state in as much as the "nightly psychosis of the normal" prevents the individual from psychotic behavior in his reality coping. Astrology offers an analogy to this split between irrationality of the dream and rationality of the waking state. The similarity may be characterized not so much by delusion as by the function of keeping the individual "normal," whatever that may be, by channelizing and to a certain extent neutralizing some of the individual's more threatening id impulses. Yet the analogy has to be qualified in various directions. To the individual, astrological belief is not a spontaneous expression of his mental life, not "his own" as much of the dream content is but is as it were, ready-made, carefully prepared and predigested irrationality. Thus far, the term "dream factory" applied to the movies applies also to astrology. It is precisely this predigested

THE STARS DOWN TO EARTH

character of astrology which produces its appearance of being normal and socially accepted and tends to obliterate the borderline between the rational and the irrational that is generally so marked with regard to dream and waking. Much like cultural industry, astrology tends to do away with the distinction of fact and fiction: its content is often overrealistic while suggesting attitudes which are based on an entirely irrational source, such as the advice to forbear entering into business ventures on some particular day. Though astrology does not have as wild an appearance as dreams or delusions, it is just this fictitious reasonableness that allows delusional urges to make their inroad into real life without overtly clashing with ego controls. Irrationality is covered up very carefully. Most of the raw material coped with as well as the advice tendered by astrological sources are extremely down-to-earth. In fact too much so, but their synthesis, the law according to which the reasonable attitudes are applied to "realistic situations," is arbitrary and entirely opaque. This may be an adequate description of the configuration of the rational and the irrational in astrology which is actually the object of this study. The confusion of these elements is also likely to define the potential danger represented by astrology as a mass phenomenon.

It is a moot point whether people who fall for astrology show, as it was taken for granted by Simmel, a psychotic predisposition, whether "psychotic characters" are especially easy to be caught by it. It may apply to the psychotic element in the normal as well and not require any special psychological susceptibility such as so-called ego weakness. In fact quite a few astrology addicts seem to enjoy a rather strong ego in terms of reality functioning. The lack of manifestly delusional content, as well as the collective backing of astrology makes it comparatively easy for the "normal" to embrace the apocryphal creed. It should also be noted that quite a few disciples of astrology accept it with a kind of mental reservation, a certain playfulness which tolerantly acknowledges its basic irrationality and their own aberration. Yet the fact that people "choose" astrology – which is not presented to them as natural as religion is to traditionally brought up persons, but requires some initiative on the adept's part – somehow indicates a lack of intellectual integration which may be partly due to the opaqueness of today's social world calling for intellectual short-cuts and partly also to expanding semi-erudition.

The ready-made "alienated" character of astrology, however, should not lead us to the oversimplification that it is something entirely ego-alien. As a psychological device adopted by the individual, astrology is in some respects reminiscent of the symptoms of the phobic neurotic which channelize, focus and absorb his free-floating anxiety seemingly in

50

terms of objects of reality. However, in phobias, no matter how rigidly structured, this channelization is by necessity impermanent and fluctuating. A phobia uses existent objects for the individual's own psychological needs. The realistic object of commercial astrology is specifically conceived and constructed in order to satisfy those psychological needs that astrologists assume to exist in their audience. In both cases, the psychological gain is extremely questionable in so far as it tends to hide actual circumstances and obstructs true recognition and correction. Interest in astrology, like a phobic symptom, may well absorb all other anxiety objects and may ultimately become an obsessive interest of the afflicted individual or group.

THE UNDERLYING PSYCHOLOGY

In contrast to the magazines, an astrological columnist like Carroll Righter faces a more vaguely defined, but presumably larger number of people with divergent interests and worries who are attracted by the column and often seek some advice. The latter has to be of such a nature that it gives *per se* some vicarious aid and comfort to the readers who can hardly be expected to be really helped by the columnist. He knows neither the persons he addresses nor the specific nature of the wishes and complaints of any of them.[9] Yet his position of authority forces him to talk as if he knew and as if the constellations of the stars provided him with satisfactory, sufficient and unequivocal answers. He can neither afford to disappoint his readers by not committing himself at all nor to compromise his magical authority on which his sales value rests by blatantly false statements. He has to face the squaring of the circle. What he says must sound as though he had concrete knowledge of what problems beset each of his prospective followers born under some sign at a specific time. Yet he must always remain non-committal enough so that he cannot be easily discredited.

While being compelled to take some chances, he tries to reduce the danger of failure to a minimum. This explains the usage of some rather rigid stereotypes of style: e.g., he frequently employs expressions such as "Follow up that intuition of yours," or "Display that keen mind of yours." The word "that" seems to imply that the columnist, on the basis of astrological inspiration, knows exactly what the individual addressee who happens to read the column is like or was like at some particular time. Yet the apparently specific references are always so general that they can be made to fit all the time: everyone has some hunch or idea on any given day or may in retrospect flatter himself by thinking that he had

51

one, and everyone, particularly the semi-erudite, would gladly accept being characterized as the owner of a keen mind. Thus, the paradox of the column is solved by the makeshift of pseudo-individualization.[10]

But such nice little tricks alone do not dispense with the columnist's fundamental difficulty. He generally has to rely on his knowledge of the most frequently recurring problems prescribed by the set-up of modern life and of characterological patterns he had frequent occasion to observe. He figures out a number of typical situations in which a large percentage of his followers might at any time find themselves. He must especially concentrate on apparently ferreting out those problems, which the reader cannot solve by his own power and force him to look for outside help, and must not even shrink from questions which are difficult to solve rationally at all so that an irrational source of advice is sought, for it is presumably precisely from such situations that people turn to the column. This leads quite logically to the fact that the astrologist's advice reflects a number of more or less insoluble situations of the present phase, impasses which threaten each individual and stimulate each individual's hopes for some effective interference from above. Even within the framework of ubiquitous problems, however, a certain latitude of expression has to be maintained so that even truly unrealistic predictions and advice can still be reconciled to the reader's life situation and are not too easily discarded. In this respect the astrologist relies on a habit equally well-known to serious psychiatrists and to popular psychologists. People who have any affinity at all to occultism are usually prepared to react to the information they are craving in such a way as to make it fit their own system at almost any cost. Thus, he even might expose himself on a factual level unpunished so long as he figures out adequately those particular needs and wishes of his readers which are so strong that they are not likely to be shattered by confrontation with reality, provided only such confrontation is really on a purely intellectual level and does not subject the readers to dire consequences in their practical life. In fact, great care is taken by the columnist to avoid this while lavishing gratifications in the realm of the imaginary.

In order to fulfill such exacting tasks, the columnist really has to be what is called in American slang, a homespun philosopher. It is perhaps this requirement which makes for the striking similarity between the column and its psychological counterparts. In this popular psychology, though shaped as it is primarily in terms of mass appeal, the knowledge of the phenomena as such, is often pertinent and the descriptions adequate. But their dynamic interpretation is either completely absent or faked: most of the time vulgar, pre-Freudian ego-psychology cloaked in what Theodor Reik has called the social workers' lingo of psycho-analese.[11] This attitude of popular psychological writings is not merely due to a lack of erudition. Since the columnist, even if he were equipped with a complete knowledge of Freud, cannot hope to change psycho-dynamically any of those to whom he speaks, he has to keep within the external zones of the personality. What really distinguishes "world-wise" institutions such as the column from real psychology is not so much observations and possibly not even the columnist's underlying inter-pretations, but the direction in which he moves and manipulates his reader's psychology. He continuously strengthens defenses rather than shatters them. He plays on the unconscious rather than attempting its elucidation beyond the most superficial phraseology.

He caters above all to *narcissism* as one of the strongest and most easily approached defenses. Often his references to his readers' outstanding qualities and chances seem so silly that it is hard to imagine that anyone will swallow them, but the columnist is well aware of the fact that vanity is nourished by so powerful instinctual sources that he who plays up to it gets away with almost anything.

Complementary to the narcissistic gratifications aimed at by the column is a more or less veiled suggestion of *anxiety*. The idea that the reader is somehow threatened must be maintained because only if some mild terror is exercised, he will seek help – analogous to advertising of drugs against body odor. Threat and relief are somehow intertwined in a way that can be spotted in various kinds of mental disorders. The kind of popular psychology on which the column relies takes it frequently for granted that most persons feel threatened, either in reality or at least psychologically, and that the column reaches them only if it establishes an intelligence with the reader in the zone of threat. Yet the threat must always be mild in order not to really shock the reader who would give up looking into a column which caused direct discomfort. Thus one of the most widely spread realistic threats, that of being fired, appears only in a diluted form, e.g., as conflicts with higher-ups, being "dressed down," and similar unpleasantnesses. The term "firing" is not used a single time.

A favorite threat, however, is that of traffic accidents. Here again one finds how various facets of the approach are blended: the danger of traffic accidents is ever-present in the congested Los Angeles area. But it is singled out as if some specific prophetic knowledge were behind it, a claim that cannot easily be refuted due to the ubiquity of the threat itself. At the same time, a threat like that of a traffic accident does not hurt the readers' narcissism on account of the complete externalization of the threat. It has hardly any humiliating implications, public opinion does not brand the traffic sinner as a criminal. Finally, reference to this threat displays one of the most prominent features of the column: supposedly irrational and magical forebodings are translated into the advice of being sensible. The stars are invoked in order to reinforce the harmless, beneficial but trivial admonition: "Drive carefully!"

Only very rarely examples turn up of more sinister threats such as that one has to be particularly careful in everything on one particular day unless one would incur serious risks.

> Ridding life of sinister acquaintance makes more assets obtainable.
>   (19 November 1952, Scorpio)

In such moments the authoritarian whip cracks down, but it does so merely as a reminder in order to keep the readers at bay, and is never carried so far as to seriously distract from the gratifications they otherwise get from the column or to make them feel uncomfortable for more than the present moment. To get rid of an acquaintance seems, after all, not too great a sacrifice or too heavy a task.

The gains the reader obtains in this particular area consist, apart from the potentiality of deep underlying gratifications to destructive urges provided by the threat itself, in the promise of help and mitigation, granted by a superhuman agency. While the subject has to follow closely what this agency indicates, he does not really have to act on his own behalf as an autonomous human being, but can content himself with relying on fate. He has to avoid things rather than to do them. He is somewhat relieved of his responsibility.

This indicates the most important construct of the column – that of readers who are or feel themselves to be basically *dependent*, who find themselves incessantly in situations which they cannot cope with by their own powers and who are beset psychologically by what has come to be known as ego weakness, but is often expressive of weakness in reality. The columnist figures quite reasonably that only the persons thus characterized are likely to rely on him unquestioningly and therefore calculates his every word in order to fit with the specific needs of the dependent – including those narcissistic defences which help them to compensate for their feelings of weakness. This again is in harmony with that kind of popular psychology whose favorite term is "inferiority complex." The columnist is quite familiar with certain forms of reaction likely to be encountered among the readers, but carefully refrains from elucidating them and thus changing them, but utilizes them in order to fixate the reader to the "message" and thus to the column as an institution. By systematic pursuit of this procedure he tends to spread the pattern of dependence and to transform more and more people into dependent ones with whom he establishes what might properly be called a situation of secondary transference.

The problem of the relation of certain neurotic traits to reality which is here implied involves grave methodological problems which can only be mentioned. Some revisionists such as Fromm and particularly Horney have oversimplified the matter by reducing neurotic traits such as the one here under consideration, dependence, to social realities such as "our modern competitive society." Since characterological patterns are likely to be established much earlier than a child makes the specific experience of a highly differentiated social system, the etiology postulated by these writers seems to be doubtful and indicative of a relapse into pre-Freudian, rationalistic psychology. At the same time, however, it is equally dubious to sever psychodynamics altogether from its "social stage." Suffice it to say here that neurotic syndromes and irrational susceptibilities of every kind are present within a large number of people at any time, but that some of them are worked upon specifically during certain periods and that modern mass media tend particularly to fortify reaction formations and defences concomitant with actual social dependence. The link between the compulsive elements of the column and the underlying idea of the subject's dependence may very well be that compulsive systems are employed as defenses against "realistic" dependence without ever involving any behavior that might change the basic situation of dependence.

It should be noted that the threat-help pattern of the column is closely related to devices more generally spread through contemporary mass culture. Hertha Herzog has pointed out in her study "On Borrowed Experience"[12] that the women's daytime serials or soap operas generally follow the formula "getting into trouble and out again," a device which incidentally seems also to be valid for jazz which constantly employs and resolves some kind of "jam." This formula is equally applicable to the astrological column. While there are continuous hints of conflict and unpleasantness, it implies that whoever is aware of these situations will somehow be taken care of.

There is a soothing overtone to the whole column: it seems to reassure the reader incessantly that "everything will be fine," overcoming his apprehensions by establishing some magical confidence in the good turn of events.

... just keep your aims high, your goals clearly before you; then all's well.

(21 November, Pisces)

55

Remainder of day splendid in practically all ways.
(6 December, Leo)
... unless you realize that in the afternoon all tension will dissolve
into happy feeling.
(31 December, Aries)

Within this general pattern of the happy ending, however, there is a
specific difference of function between the column and other mass
communications. Soap operas, television shows and above all movies are
characterized by heroes, persons who positively or negatively solve their
own problems. They stand vicariously for the spectator. By identifying
himself with the hero, he believes to participate in the very power that is
denied him in as much as he conceives himself as weak and dependent.
While the column also works with identifications, they are organized
differently. There are no heroic figures in the column, and only general
hints of charismatic persons such as the mysterious creative and powerful
people from outside who occasionally crop up and tender the reader
invaluable aid. By and large, people are taken for what they are. True,
their social status is, as will be demonstrated later, vicariously raised by
the column, but their problems are not hidden behind an imagery of
ruggedness or irresistibility – in this respect, the column seems more
realistic than the supposedly artistic mass media.

For the column, the hero is replaced by either the heavenly signs or,
more likely, by the omniscient columnist himself. Since the course of
events is referred to as to something pre-established, people will not have
the feeling, still present in hero worship, that by identification with the
hero, they may have to be heroic themselves. Their problems will be
solved either automatically or with the help of others, particularly of
those mysterious friends whose image recurs throughout the column,
provided one only proves confident in the stars. Impersonal power thus
replaces the personalized one of the heroes and is transferred to his more
powerful superiors. It is as if the column would try to make up by its
identification with the reader's actual psychological and reality situation
of dependence for the unrealistic element of the dogmatic reference to
the stars. The column indulges in a symbolic expression and psychological fortification of the pressure that is being continuously exercised
upon people. They are simply to have confidence in that which is
anyway. Fate, while being exalted as a metaphysical power, actually
denotes the interdependence of anonymous social forces through which
the people addressed by the column will somehow "muddle through."
The semi-irrationality of "everything will be fine" is based on the fact

that modern American society in spite of all its conflicts and difficulties succeeds in reproducing the life of those whom it embraces. There is some dim awareness that the concept of the forgotten man is outdated. The column feeds on this awareness by teaching the readers not to be afraid of being weak. They are reassured that all their problems will solve themselves even if they feel that they themselves are unable to solve them. They are made to understand – and in a way rightly – that the very same powers by which they are threatened, the anonymous totality of the social process, are also those which will somehow take care of them. Thus they are trained to identify themselves with the existent *in abstracto* rather than with heroic persons, to concede their own impotence and thus be allowed as a compensation to go on living without too much worrying. This promise, of course, is contingent upon their being "good boys" (or girls) who behave according to given standards, but who also allow themselves, for therapeutic reasons, as it were, that range of pleasure which they need in order not to collapse under the requirements of reality, or under the impact of their own urges.

It goes without saying that this is a remedy ultimately as problematic as the remedy offered by the movies though it may not be so obviously spurious. Life actually does not automatically take care of people. But it does to a certain extent and where it doesn't, insecurity and threats make people susceptible to unfounded promises. They do not only play a role in the individual's psychological household, but also fulfill the function of a conservative ideology, generally justifying the *status quo*. An order of existence which expresses the promise to take care of everyone, must be substantially good. Thus the column promotes social conformity in a deeper and more comprehensive sense than merely by inducing con-formist behavior from case to case. It creates an atmosphere of social contentment.

This explains an outstanding peculiarity of the individual advice tendered by the column. It implies that all problems due to objective circumstances such as, above all, economic difficulties, can be solved in terms of private individual behavior or by psychological insight, particularly into oneself, but also into others.

This is indicative of a function popular psychology is nowadays assuming to an ever-increasing extent. While psychology, when really carried through, is a medium of insight into oneself, criticism of oneself and concomitantly insight and criticism of others, it can also play the role of a social drug. In particular, objective difficulties which doubtlessly always have their subjective aspects and are partly rooted in the subjects, are presented as though they were completely due to the individual.[13]

This alleviates any critical attitude, even that towards oneself, since the individual is provided with the narcissistic gratification that he is really all-important while at the same time being kept under control. While the world is not so bad, he is given to understand that somehow problems arise within his behavior and action alone. Finding the right approach to himself is regarded as sufficient condition for relieving all difficulties, thus partly making up for the feeling of weakness from which the whole approach starts. The pat formula "everything depends on man" is not only a half truth, but really serves to cloak everything that materializes over the heads of people.

The column contains all the elements of reality and somehow catches the actual state of affairs but nevertheless constructs a distorted picture. On the one hand, the objective forces beyond the range of individual psychology and individual behavior are exempt from critique by being endowed with metaphysical dignity. On the other hand, one has nothing to fear from them if one only follows objective configurations through a process of adaptation. Thus the danger seems to lie exclusively within the power of the powerless individual whose superego is continuously appealed to.

> Urge to tell off official would alienate helpful partner, so keep calm despite irritation: later material benefits will follow making more cooperative deal at home.
> (10 November, Aries)
> Sulking over disappointing act of influential executive merely puts you deeper in disfavor.
> (10 November, Scorpio)
> Get away from that concern that seems to have no solution.
> (10 November, Sagittarius)
> Your own A.M. fretfulness and lack of vision alone makes the morning unsatisfactory.
> (11 November, Libra)

The constant appeal of the column to find fault with oneself rather than with given conditions, a subtle but highly objectionable modification of an element of modern depth-psychology, is only one aspect of the ideal of social *conformity*, promoted throughout the column and expressed by the implicit, but ubiquitous rule that one has to adjust oneself continuously to commands of the stars at a given time. While the problems of the individual spotted by the column denote, no matter how diluted and weak, areas in which everything is not well and in which the official optimism promulgated by the column meets some difficulties, the description of these problems and particularly the subsequent advice fulfill the function of re-establishing the established order, of enforcing conformity and keeping securely within the existent. Our asserting that the irrationality of the fate that dictates everything and of the stars that offer advice is really but a screen for society which both threatens the individual and grants it its livelihood is borne out by the messages derived from the irrational source. They are indeed nothing but messages from the social *status quo* in the way it is conceived by the column. *The over-all rule of the column is to enforce the requirements society makes on each individual so that it might "function."* The more irrational the requirements, the more they call for irrational justifications. Problems arising out of social conditions and antagonisms are reconciled by the column with social conventionality, and in this aim, threat and help converge. The column consists of an incessant battery of appeals to be "reasonable." If the "unreasonable," i.e., instinctual urges, are admitted at all, it is only for the sake of reasonableness, namely in order to make the individual function better according to the rules of conformity.

It has been noted in the discussion of the astrological magazines that their basic irrationality never leads to any renunciations of the normal, rational way of everyday behavior. This attitude, which, in the magazines, is complementary to sometimes wild fantasies, is the exclusive medium of the column. It strikes an unquestioning common-sense attitude, stresses accepted values and takes it for granted that this is a "competitive world" – whatever this may mean today – and that the only thing that really counts is success. Anything approaching the irresponsible is shunned, no connotation of the crank is tolerated. Here again the column is in harmony with cultural industry as a whole. The customary reference to "dream factory," nowadays employed by the representatives of the movie industry themselves, contains only a half truth – it pertains only to the overt "dream content." The message of the dream, however, the "latent dream idea" as promoted by motion pictures and television reverses that of actual dreams. It is an appeal to agencies of psychological control rather than an attempt to unfetter the unconscious. The idea of the successful, conforming, well-adjusted "average" citizen lurks even behind the fanciest technicolor fairy tale. Astrology is no exception to that rule. It does not teach its followers anything to which they are not accustomed by their daily experience; it only reinforces what they have been taught anyway consciously and unconsciously. The stars seem to be in complete agreement with the established ways of life and with the habits and institutions circumscribed by our age. The adage "be yourself" assumes an ironical meaning. The socially manipulated stimuli constantly aim at reproducing that frame of mind which is spontaneously engendered by the *status quo* itself. This attitude which would appear, if viewed merely rationalistically, as a "waste of effort," is actually in line with psychological findings. Freud has stated repeatedly and emphatically that the effectiveness of psychological defenses is always of a precarious nature. If the satisfaction of instinctual urges is denied or postponed, they are rarely kept under reliable control, but are most of the time ready to break through if they find a chance. This readiness to break through is enhanced by the problematic nature of the rationality that recommends postponement of immediate wish-fulfillment for the sake of later permanent and complete gratifications. One is taught to give up immediate pleasures for the sake of a future which only too often fails to compensate for the pleasures one has renounced. Thus rationality does not always seem as rational as it claims to be. Hence the interest of hammering over and over again into people's heads ideas to which they are already conditioned but in which they can never fully believe. Hence also their readiness to embrace irrational panaceas in a world in which they have lost faith in the effectiveness of their own reason and in the rationality of the total set-up.

IMAGE OF THE ADDRESSEE

Perusal of the column over a longer period of time permits one to figure out the columnist's image of his reader, the basis of the techniques he employs. The over-all rule is that this picture must mainly be flattering, offer gratifications even before actual advice is tendered, but must be at the same time of such a nature that the addressee can still identify himself and his petty worries with the picture of himself he is constantly offered.

No American data were available as to the sex distribution of astrology fans, but it seems reasonable to assume that their majority are women or at least that women are equally represented among them. The columnist is very likely well aware of this. Strangely enough, however, the implicit picture of the addressee, though rarely quite articulate, is predominantly male. The reader is presented as a professional person who has authority and has to make decisions; he is presented as a practical person, technically minded and able to fix things. Most characteristic of all, whenever the erotic sphere is touched upon, the addressee has to see an "attractive companion." As a popular psychologist, the columnist seems to be better aware than many supposedly serious writers of the inferior status of women in modern society in spite of their supposed emancipation, their participation in professional life and the glamor heaped upon some of them. He seems to feel that women will usually feel flattered if they are treated as men as long as the specific sphere of their femininity and its conventional attributes are not involved which does not happen in the column; it is suggested to each housewife that she might be a V.I.P. Possibly the columnist draws even on some psycho-analytic knowledge of penis envy[14] when talking to an audience of women as though he were addressing men.

An additional factor may be contributing to the male characterization of the addressee. Since the column is continuously tendering advice, wants people to act and takes the over-all attitude of the "practical," it appears necessary to speak as though one would address those who really act, the decision makers – men. The more women are actually dependent, on a deeper level, the more important it may be to them that they are treated as though they were the ones on whom everything depended though actually the treatment they are given by the column to which they are tied really enhances their own dependence.

The standard image is that of a young person or one in his early thirties, vigorous in his professional pursuits, given to hearty pleasures which must somehow be held in check and prone to romance – rather a subtle gratification to presumably frustrated readers who are likely to identify themselves with the addressee if born under the astrological sign mentioned and transfer the imaginary addressee's qualities upon themselves.

The addressee belongs to some church though no reference is made to which denomination and no specific dogma is ever expressed or mentioned. But it is taken for granted that he attends some service on Sunday as a "regular" person and a solemn semi-religious tone is usually reserved for holidays. The image of religion is entirely conventionalized. Religious activities are restricted to leisure time and the reader is encouraged to attend some "good sermon," as though he were to select a show.

> Fine for inexpensive entertaining, sports, recreation, romance.
> Attend worship, then keep living religion.
>   (14 December 1952, Cancer)
> Routine tasks seem dreary. Forget them. Go to church where you
> can find better religious ideas that are able to support your many
> burdens.
>   (28 December 1952, Capricorn)

The addressee is sometimes presented as a car owner. Whereas this seems realistic enough in view of the tremendous number of car owners in greater Los Angeles, even here some cuddling might be involved in as much as one might expect to find among the devoted readers of the column quite a few persons who do not own cars but like the idea that they are treated as though they did.

It should also be noted that no reference to the addressee's educational level is made. Whenever his personal qualities are summoned, they are either completely severed from what he might have learned, stressing merely "gifts" such as charm, "magnetism," etc., or they pertain vaguely to his family background. But it does not make any difference whether the addressee went through college, through high school or only to grammar school. This might be indicative of the fact that the columnist's real image of the addressee differs significantly from the one he promotes. While he evinces the idea that the addressee is a superior person he is very careful not to draw a picture of this superiority which would be definite enough to alienate the reader by making him aware that he does not fit the picture at all.

By far the most important feature of the addressee is his socio-economic status. The image presented in this area may be called, with some exaggeration, that of the *vice-president*. The people spoken to are pictured as holding a superior place in life which forces them, as mentioned before, to make decisions all the time. Much depends on them, on their reasonableness, their ability to make up their minds. It is carefully avoided to represent them in so many words as impotent or unimportant small men. One may think of the well-known technique of magazines such as *Fortune* which are written to give the impression that each of their presumably very numerous readers were a big shot in some major corporation. The vicarious gratification thus provided, the strong appeal exercised by the transference of the American ideal of the successful businessman upon the none-too-successful is obvious. Yet – and this is why the column addresses vice-presidents rather than presidents – the reality situation is never lost sight of. Whereas the illusion of importance and autonomy is superficially kept intact, the fact is not forgotten that these much desired assets are really not being fully enjoyed by the addressee. He is therefore presented as someone who although fairly high himself in the business hierarchy has essentially to depend on others who are even higher. Since this may be the situation even of some real vice-presidents, the feeling of humiliation is somewhat attenuated at the same time. Advice can be proffered that befits the underling without revealing that he really is an underling although on a deeper level he may very well be made to understand that he has only little to say. The addressee's ego ideal and his realistic experience of his actual place in life are somehow fused. At the same time, the hierarchical way of thinking often to be met among compulsive[15] lower middle-class people is met halfway.

Treating the addressee as an important link in the hierarchy is indicative of one of the basic psychological constructs of the addressee suggested by the set-up of the column. While he is figured out probably quite realistically as a basically weak and dependent person both with regard to his actual function in the social set-up and to his psychological characteristics, he is not likely to admit his weakness and dependence. This defense is taken into account as much as the dependency needs themselves. Hence, the reactive picture of themselves developed by dependent people is strengthened. Here belongs, above all, hyperactivity. Continuous advice is given to take some action, to behave like a successful go-getter. What is thus emphasized is not so much the addressee's real ego power as his intellectual identification with some socialized ego ideal. He is led to interpret his actions as though he were strong and as though his activity would amount to something. The phoniness of this concept is indicated by the spuriousness of most of the activities encouraged by the column. "Pseudo-activity,"[16] a very widespread behavioral pattern in our society, is represented rather clearly by the column and the psychological calculations on which it is based.

It would be one-sided, however, to reduce the psychological image of the addressee entirely to categories such as dependence and ego weakness and the infantile fixation specifically involved – orality.[17] The columnist is by no means committed to these categories which, particularly as far as ego weakness is concerned, would be inadequate even for a popular psychologist. The underlying ideas of the psychology of the addressees are much more polymorphous. The columnist starts from the generalized assumption that his readers are regressive, warped persons, and all the major dimensions of regression actually involved in most defects of intellect and personality, are somehow taken care of and catered to. In order to understand how this works, one will have to distinguish between the image of the addressee, which is projected by the columnist, and the columnist's real underlying estimate of his readers. While he creates the addressee in the image of the big shot with some worries, he reckons with an average lower-middle-class reader. Throughout psychoanalytic literature down to its current popularization, the affinity between the lower-middle-class mentality and certain infantile fixations has been recognized. Even the popular psychologist today has heard that the petty bourgeois is likely to be an anal character.[18] While the column neglects quite a few of the implications of anality such as sadism and stinginess (they are incompatible with the synthetic ego ideal it promotes), the more general pattern of anality, and one of the most widespread of retrogressive personalities, is underscored the more heavily: compulsiveness.

It is intrinsic to the astrological pattern itself: one believes he has to obey some highly systematized orders without, however, any manifest interconnection between the system and himself. In astrology as in compulsive neurosis, one has to keep very strictly to some rule, command or advice without ever being able to say why. It is just this "blindness" of obedience which seems to be fused with the over-whelming and frightening power of the command. In as much as the stars as viewed in astrology form an intricate system of do's and don't's, this system seems to be the projection of a compulsive system itself.

Just as advice from the stars enhances irrational authoritarian dependence and submissiveness, reference to inscrutable and inexorable laws which one somehow has to imitate by one's own rigid behavior strengthens the compulsive potential with the addressee. Numerous recommendations of the column which make a major affair of the painstakingly strict fulfillment of requirements and tasks which are actually meaningless and have very little influence on reality are plainly encouraging compulsive behavior. There are innumerable passages like the following ones:

In P.M. more charm in environment brings desired peace.
(11 November 1952, Sagittarius)
Your own day to take those beauty treatments, get haircuts, do whatever increases your personal charm and sense of well-being.
(13 November 1952, Libra)
In P.M. arrange cleaning, laundry, clothing, furnishing, diet problems.
(November 1952, Virgo)

This is one of the major demonstrations of the fact that the psychological insight on the part of the columnist is not utilized in order to really develop psychological insight on the part of the reader but rather in the opposite direction, in order to maintain his defenses and to fixate him to irrational patterns, thus making him more obedient to the columnist, the self-styled spokesman of social norms. The underlying idea of compulsive behavior (if he fulfills this or that unpleasant duty, it will liberate him from guilt feelings and earn him some sort of compensation) is directly reflected by the logic of the column. It should be stressed, however, that just as in the case of dependence, even here a realistic element is not altogether absent. Just as the exploitation of the addressee's susceptibility to psychological dependence exploits his truly dependent status in society, the compulsive traits worked out by the column are frequently those which are expected of those persons who are likely to believe in the column's revelations. To overrate the importance of fulfilling mechanical chores, may be a symptom of compulsive neurosis, but the little fellow who has no space for "creative" or spontaneous activities and who is expected to function as a cog in a bureaucratic machinery, must do his chores strictly and conscientiously, nothing less, but also nothing more. In fact, if he were to try to do more, he might be suspected as an "apple polisher" or as having big ideas in his head, as mal-adjusted to his job and might be fired. Realistic considerations of this kind are thoroughly blended by the column with psychological lore.

Nevertheless, the "realism" in the addressee served so punctiliously by the advice of the column, is never entirely realistic. The overemphasis on realism in the actual content of the column is also calculated to make the addressee forget the irrationality of the whole system about which one should not think too much, whereas the almost complete absence of any hint at the sources of advice tendered therein mirrors the severe repression that always works upon the instincts of the compulsive. Nowhere is the relationship between realism and its counterpart so hard to distinguish as in the area of compulsiveness.

THE BI-PHASIC APPROACH

It has been mentioned before that the column aims at promoting conventional, conformist and contented attitudes and that any insights into negative aspects of reality are kept under control by making everything dependent on the individual rather than on objective conditions. The individual is promised the solution to everything if he complies with certain requirements and avoids certain negative stereotypes. He is prevented from really acknowledging the very same difficulties which drive him into the arms of astrology. But the column is much too well aware of the seriousness of reality problems as well as of psychological ones to rely entirely on the effectiveness of its own ideology. It has to face people who find out from life experience continuously that everything does not run so smooth as the column seems to imply it does and that not everything takes care of itself. They are incessantly beset by irreconcilable and contradictory requirements or their own psychological economy as well as of social reality: the column constructs its addressee as being "frustrated." It does not suffice to the column to simply deny the existence of these requirements and to comfort the frustrated; somehow the column has to take up these contradictions themselves if it really wants to tie the readers to its own authority. It fulfills this task which by necessity cannot be solved by the mere promulgation of a "positive" ideology, nor by any other content that could be easily refuted by everyday facts, rather ingeniously by its formal set-up, thus fortifying an otherwise precarious balance of contradictory requirements, in the reader.

The basic formal device employed here, and probably the most effective trick of the column as a whole, is derived from its principal medium, i.e., the *time* element. Astrology pretends basically that the stars determine what will happen or, if the approach is brought more "up-to-date," what is advisable or inadvisable at any given day or hour. Thus frequently a certain general mood is maintained for a whole day, supposedly due to the basic constellations of this day, affecting every reader, no matter under which sign he may have been born. Here is the "Astrological Forecast" for Sunday 20 November 1952:

ARIES (21 March to 19 April): A.M. bring many problems into open to test your self-control, ideas to be lived in daily tasks; P.M. your mind solves them, finds new avenues in which growth, expansion excellent.

TAURUS (20 April to 20 May): You have a good chance A.M. to think deeply into unusual ways to push ahead. P.M. dynamic official brings you chance to add to your revenue; show appreciation by trying suggestions.

GEMINI (21 May to 21 June): A.M. finds you able to solve quietly present riddles in your way of life; discuss with understanding individual. P.M. splendid for forging ahead to new goals awaiting you all ways.

CANCER (22 June to 21 July): Early A.M. feeling of wellbeing starts interesting day right; attend worship as your chosen outlet for expanding happiness; P.M. keep companions jolly by entertaining.

LEO (22 July to 21 August): Seek those early who lift your spirits, bring you solace; forget the humdrum in enjoying others; P.M. get together with friends, partners, for amusements, romance, sports.

VIRGO (22 August to 22 September): Listen carefully to what both friends, attachments suggest in lines improving conditions at home, with family; P.M. organize calendar to use good coming week wisely.

LIBRA (23 September to 22 October): Calm hurt feelings of family, others important to your life, A.M., let them talk grievances out of their systems; P.M. enjoy neighbors, relatives, close associates; be charming.

SCORPIO (23 October to 21 November): You have chance to coordinate higher ideals in everyday living by careful A.M. study; P.M. much activity at home brings into open improved plans for financial security.

SAGITTARIUS (22 November to 21 December): Doing job with routines thoroughly, avoiding costly commitments A.M. brings peace, contentment; P.M. use all that mental energy generated to improve all your affairs.

CAPRICORN (22 December to 20 January): Refusal to allow upset comrade to disturb your equanimity great assistance A.M. to all about; P.M. quietly look to present practical interests; plan to improve coming week.

AQUARIUS (21 January to 19 February): Side-step those routine tasks that make you want to explode A.M., contact, enjoy good friends instead; P.M. use all that vitality to arrange new plan for attaining goals.

PISCES (20 February to 20 March): Morning fine for seeking out good friends, loved ones, making plans to have good time later; P.M. making secret arrangements to bring your talents to one able to aid is best.

This establishes, first of all, the supremacy of time, but does not yet take care of conflicting requirements. However, this all important task, too, is shifted upon time. It has to fulfill the role of the ultimate decision maker.

The problem how to disperse with contradictory requirements of life is solved by the simple device of distributing these requirements over different periods mostly of the same day. The fact that one cannot countenance two contradictory desires at the same time, that, as it is loosely called, one cannot have one's cake and eat it too, induces the advice that irreconcilable activities simply should be undertaken at various times indicated by celestial configurations. This again feeds on realistic elements: the order of everyday life takes care of a number of antinomies of existence, such as that of work and leisure or of public functions and private existence. Such antinomies are taken up by the column, hypostatized and treated as though they were simple dichotomies of the natural order of things rather than sociologically conditioned patterns. Everything can be solved, so runs the implicit argument, if one only chooses the right time, and if one fails, this is merely due to a lack of understanding of some supposedly cosmic rhythm. This indeed achieves a kind of equilibrium and satisfaction that cannot be achieved if the contradictions are faced as such, i.e., as simultaneous and equally potent demands by various psychological or outside agencies. They are all replaced by the more abstract but less offensive and affect-laden time concept. Thus, A.M., comprising the bulk of the work day, is frequently treated as representative of reality and the ego principle: people are advised to be particularly reasonable during the morning.

> Tax problems, money dealings with others easily attended to in morning.
>> (Saturday, 15 November 1952, Taurus)
> Looking straight at present obligations, duties, restrictions early shows right way to solve them simply and effectively.
>> (16 November 1952, Sagittarius)
> Keep smiling plodding at chosen tasks despite early A.M. feeling nothing works right. Plan different clever methods quietly.
>> (2 December 1952, Leo)
> A.M. brings big chance to iron out any concerns regarding officials, executives, career, credits.
>> (15 December 1952, Taurus)
> A.M. finds many little duties that you'd best do early, freeing remainder of the day for much joy.
>> (1 January 1953, Virgo)
> Early desire for fun can put a big dent in bankroll, so be economical.
>> (2 January 1953, Aries)
> A.M. finds your own desires conflicting with those of family member. Don't argue, cooperate to prevent lasting resentment.
>> (2 January 1953, Taurus)

Conversely, P.M., which generally includes at least a certain amount of leisure time, is handled as though it were the representative of the instinctual urges of the pleasure principle:[19] people are often admonished to seek pleasure, particularly the "simple pleasures of life," to wit, the gratifications offered by other mass media during the afternoon or evening.

> Afternoon finds pleasures all about: enjoy thoroughly; relax in P.M.
>> (16 November 1952, Virgo)

P.M. get out from present preoccupations; entertain; enjoy sports, romance.
(17 November, Leo)
A.M. finds need for secret huddle with member of family to eliminate present worry; later excellent influences prevail for you to enjoy amusements, romance, recreation.
(19 November 1952, Virgo)
In P.M. enjoy sports, romance, entertainment, recreation.
(21 November 1952, Libra)
P.M. enjoy pleasures, recreation, love.
(23 November 1952, Leo)

By dichotomies of this kind a pseudo-solution of difficulties is achieved: either–or relationships are transformed into first–next relationships. Pleasure thus becomes the award of work, work the atonement for pleasure.

While this formal scheme of the column is derived from its medium and mirrors the time schedule to which most people are subject, it is again very shrewdly keyed to psychological dispositions frequently encountered in stymied personalities. Here again the semi-popular concept of ego weakness first comes to mind. Erich Fromm has pointed out in his study "*Zum Gefühl der Ohnmacht*" (The Feeling of Impotence), from which we quote in a free translation:

Faith in time lacks the sense of sudden change. It substitutes expectations that 'in due time' everything will come out all right. Conflicts, which one feels unable to resolve oneself, are expected to be resolved by time without one's having to take the risk of deciding. Faith in time is found especially frequently with respect to one's own achievements. People not only console themselves over their unperformed performances, but also over not preparing for the performance by persuading themselves that they have so much time left and that there is no reason to hurry. An example of this mechanism is the case of a greatly gifted author who wanted to write a book which, in his opinion, would rank among the most important of world literature. All he did was to pursue a series of thoughts about it, to indulge in fantasies about the epoch-making effect his book would produce and to tell his friends that it was almost finished. Actually, although he had 'worked' on the book for seven years, he had not yet written a single line. As these people get older, they must cling even more stubbornly to the illusion that time will take care of things. Many, when they reach a certain age, usually the early forties, either sober up and abandon the illusion and make efforts to utilize their own powers or have a neurotic break-down because life without the consoling illusion of time as a benefactor becomes intolerable.[20]

It may be added to Fromm's remark that the tendency he describes seems to be derived from an infantile attitude, possibly related to the child's fantasies of what will happen when he is "grown up." What is at certain times realistic in children who know that they will grow and who have neither full disposal of their potential faculties nor the autonomy of making their own decisions, becomes neurotic when it is carried over into adult life. People with a weak ego or objectively incapable of molding their own fate show a certain readiness to shift their responsibility to the abstract time factor which absolves them of their failures and promotes their hope as though they could expect relief from all their ills from the very simple fact that things move on and more particularly that most sufferings are likely to be forgotten – the capacity of memory actually being linked with a strong development of the ego. This psychological disposition is both strengthened and utilized by the column which enhances the confidence in time by giving it the mystical connotation that time is somehow expressive of the verdict of the stars.

Beyond such observations, the dichotomous interpretation of time can probably be understood in depth-psychological terms. A valid interpretation of this approach is probably obtained by the concept of the bi-phasic symptoms frequent in compulsive neurosis. Fenichel describes the mechanism as follows:

> In reaction formation, an attitude is taken that contradicts the original one; in undoing, one more step is taken. Something positive is done which, actually or magically, is the opposite of something which, again actually or in imagination, was done before. This mechanism can be most clearly observed in certain compulsive symptoms that are made up of two actions, the second of which is a direct reversion of the first. For example – a patient must first turn on the gas jet and then turn it off again. All symptoms that represent expiations belong in this category, for it is the nature of expiation to annul antecedent acts. The idea of expiation itself is nothing but an expression of belief in the possibility of a magical undoing.[21]

This mechanism is related to compulsiveness:

> Whereas some compulsive symptoms are distorted modes of

perceiving instinctual demands and others express the anti-instinctual threats of the superego, still other symptoms obviously show the struggle between the two. Most of the symptoms of obsessive doubt can be covered by the formula: 'May I be naughty, or must I be good?' Sometimes a symptom consists of two phases, one representing an objectionable impulse, the other the defense against it. Freud's 'rat-man,' for instance, felt compelled to remove a stone from the road because it might hurt somebody, and then felt compelled to put it back again.[22]

What results if expiation and undoing are obsessively institutionalized is called:

> a bi-phasic behavior. The patient behaves alternately as though he were a naughty child and a strict punitive disciplinarian. For obsessive reasons a patient was not able to brush his teeth. After not brushing his teeth for a while, he would slap and scold himself. Another patient always carried a notebook, in which he would make check marks according to his conduct to indicate praise or blame.[23]

Defenses and behavior patterns of this kind while actually neurotic are systematized and presented as normal and wholesome throughout the set-up of the column. As a matter of fact, this principle of organization permeates it to such an extent that most of the specific devices now to be analyzed can and will be presented within the framework of the bi-phasic approach.

WORK AND PLEASURE

When children learn English in Germany, they are often taught as one of the first poems they are made acquainted with:

> Work while you work, play while you play.
> This is the way to be cheerful and gay.

The idea is that by strictly keeping work and pleasure apart, both ranges of activity will benefit: no instinctual aberrations will interfere with seriousness of rational behavior, no signs of seriousness and responsibility will cast their shadow over the fun. Obviously this advice is somehow derived from social organization which affects the individual in as much as his life falls into two sections, one where he functions as a producer and one where he functions as a consumer. It is as though the basic dichotomy of the economic life process of society were projected upon the individual. Psychologically, the compulsive connotations based on a puritan outlook can hardly be overlooked: not only with regard to the bi-phasic pattern of life as a whole but also to notions such as cleanliness: neither of the two spheres must be contaminated by the other. While the advice may offer advantages in terms of economic rationalization, its intrinsic merits are of a dubious nature. Work completely severed from the element of playfulness becomes drab and monotonous, a tendency which is consummated by the complete quantification of industrial work. Pleasure when equally isolated from the "serious" content of life, becomes silly, meaningless and sheer "entertainment" and ultimately it is a mere means of reproducing one's working capacity, whereas the real substance of any non-utilitarian activity lies in the way it faces and sublimates reality problems: *res severa verum gaudium.*

The complete severance of work and play as an attitudinal pattern of the total personality may justly be called a process of disintegration strangely concomitant with the integration of utilitarian operations for the sake of which this dichotomy has been introduced.

The column does not bother about such problems, but sticks to the well-established "work while you work, play while you play" advice. It thus falls in line with many phases of contemporary mass culture where maxims of the earlier development of middle-class society are repeated in a congealed form although their technological and sociological basis does not exist anymore.

The columnist is very well aware of the drudgery of most subordinate functions in a hierarchical and bureaucratic set-up and of the resistance bred in those who have to do some work which is often completely alien to their subjective urges, which can be done as well by anyone else and which may have been reduced to so small mechanical functions that it cannot possibly be regarded as meaningful. They are continuously admonished to attend to this kind of work under the flimsy pretext that this is the way to comply with the order of the day.

However, in this ideology there are some subtle significant changes in comparison with the old "work while you work" attitude. What people are supposed to do during A.M. is no longer supposed to be an auto-nomous activity molded after the model of the independent entre-preneur. Rather they are encouraged to fulfill little and insignificant set tasks in a machinery. Thus, the admonition to work and not to allow oneself to be distracted by any instinctual interference has frequently the form that one should attend to one's "*chores.*"

Dismal early A.M. forgotten by plunging into routine chores.
(21 November 1952, Leo)
Keep plugging at chores. . .
(19 December 1952, Sagittarius)
Stick to attending chores. . .
(27 December 1952, Sagittarius)

Most of the time chores are to be done right away according to such advice, occasionally – and this is characteristic of the column's mosaic technique that brings the same basic categories into various configurations – to be postponed for more suitable times.

It's unnecessary that you fuss so much with routine chores this morning.
(10 November 1952, Taurus)

The term "chores" seems to conjure up unquestioningly accepting minor tasks as a superior law, guided not by insight into their intrinsic necessity but only by fear of punishment. The column strives to overcome resistance against meaningless routine work by playing upon the compulsive libidinization that increases so often in reverse proportion to the importance of the chores.

This psychological tendency is exploited even more where the idea of minor responsibilities is carried over to private existence. Activities such as washing one's car or fixing some household contraption, inferior though they may be, are still somewhat closer to the subject's own range of interest than the business routine, for those activities pertain to what belongs to him and is regarded as part of his "ego" realm whereas he often feels that what he does in business ultimately serves only others. This observation is fused with the columnist's knowledge of the tremendous and doubtlessly irrational role of "gadgeteering" in the psychological household of many people today. Labor-saving devices, primarily necessitated by objective conditions such as the scarcity of domestic help, are invested with a halo of their own. This may be indicative of a fixation to a phase of adolescent activities in which people try to adapt themselves to modern technology by making it, as it were, their own cause. It may be mentioned in this connection that the real psychodynamics of gadgeteering are still largely unexplored and that their study would be utterly timely in order to gain insight into the emotional ties between the objective set-up of contemporary conditions and the individuals who live under these conditions. It seems that the kind of retrogression highly characteristic of persons who do not any longer feel they are the self-determining subjects of their fate, is concomitant with a fetishistic attitude towards the very same conditions which tend to be dehumanizing them. The more they are gradually being transformed into things, the more they invest things with a human aura. At the same time, the libidinization of gadgets is indirectly narcissistic in as much as it feeds on the ego's control of nature: gadgets provide the subject with some memories of early feelings of omnipotence. Since this type of cathexis shifts from ends to means which are treated as though they were things themselves, a close affinity to concretism can be observed. This is given away in the column by occasional rather eccentric statements such as "buy interesting gadgets."

> Make more happiness there (your home) by more interesting gadgets. . .
> (3 December 1952, Aquarius)

As to *pleasure*, it is, according to the bi-phasic approach, mainly reserved for P.M. and for holidays as though there were an *a priori* understanding between celestial revelations and the present calendar system. For the sake of variation and in order not to make the bi-phasic monotony too obvious, there are exceptions to the rule.

It would be erroneous, however, to assume that the bi-phasic division of work and pleasure puts both work and pleasure on an equal footing. Since the approach itself, the "division" of life into various functions which are supposed to be more productive if kept apart, is chosen under the auspices of psychological rationalization, the priority of the rational over indulgence, to put it crudely of the ego over the id, is strictly maintained. *It is one of the major tenets of the column, possibly the most important of all, that pleasure itself is permissible only if it serves ultimately some ulterior purpose of success and self-promotion.* There is a double reason for the conspicuous emphasis on this principle. On the one hand, the prevailing idea of conformity to what one is expected to do as well as the pretense to help people to master their everyday conflicts which often arise out of their resistance to routine work requires a strengthening of traditional working morals – possibly because in the present era, the more technology advances, tedious work seems to become superfluous and is therefore increasingly resented as long as it still goes on. The column has to take care of a specific social irrationality that gradually shows up today. On the other hand, the columnist knows of the guilt feelings frequently induced by pleasure. They are assuaged by making the reader understand that some pleasure is permissible in so far as it is a "release," that he would, as popular psychology has learned by now, become a neurotic person unless he allowed himself some gratifications, and above all that there are many pleasures which fulfill immediately and directly some economically gainful purpose. Since this concept of pleasure for duty's sake is contradictory in itself, again some bizarreness shows up that sheds light over the whole area covered by the column.

There is above all the monotonously frequent advice to "be happy." (Cf., for example, 27 November 1952, Scorpio; 28 November 1952, Sagittarius; 15 December 1952, Sagittarius; 16 December 1952, Leo; 23 December 1952, Sagittarius.) Obviously it is directed at encouraging the reader to overcome what, in popular psychology, has come to be known as "inhibitions." However, this encouragement becomes paradoxical in as much as instinctual needs contrary to the rule of rational interests appear to be commandeered by rational interests. Even that which is spontaneous and involuntary is being made part of arbitrariness and control. It is like a parody of the Freudian dictum that what is id would become ego. The former appears switched on, ordered, as it were, by conscience. One is forced to have fun in order to be well adjusted or at least appear so to others because only well-adjusted people are accepted as normal and are likely to be successful. One should here remember that psychological experiments have shown a high correlation between subjective sympathy with a face that has a happy look and, conversely, antipathy toward people who look unhappy. This aspect of universal externalization comes close to what has been called "fun morality" by Wolfenstein and Leites: "You've got to have fun" (whether you like it or not).[24] Instinctual requirements are freed from threatening aspects by being themselves treated as duties to be performed – the psychoanalytic concept of *Genussfähigkeit* (capacity for pleasure) already carries this fatal connotation within itself. At the same time, however, censorship is extended. Sexuality itself is being desexualized, as it were, by becoming "fun," a sort of hygiene. It loses not only its more threatening and ego-alien impact, but also its intensity, its "flavor." This tendency, clearly shown by the column, was pointed out in Aldous Huxley's *Brave New World*, where he describes orgies deteriorated into social functions; while the adage most frequently uttered by the inhabitants of his negative utopia reads *"everybody is happy nowadays."*

The semi-tolerant integration of pleasure into a rigid pattern of life is achieved by the ever-recurring promise that pleasure trips, sprees, parties and similar events will lead to practical advantages. One will make new acquaintances, build up "connections" that prove helpful for the career if one walks out with business associates. Relations may become smoother and as implied indirectly one's position may become firmer and better remunerated. Sometimes there are even hints that if one takes out one's romantic interest one might benefit from the sound business intuitions of the woman he loves.

... enjoying congenial amusement with serious comrade clears path for successful association.
(19 November 1952, Cancer)
... entertain recent new influential acquaintances.
(24 November 1952, Virgo)
... woman comrade introduces, praises you to influential friend able to push you ahead.
(26 November 1952, Cancer)
Much conversation with an official or associate, especially at a social function or sporting event, reveals your talents so that real support is quickly given.
(3 January 1953, Gemini)
It's your day to have fun; so contact very active associates, take them to amusement places, and discuss practical goals in these surroundings for excellent results.
(9 January 1952, Cancer)

In all these respects the image of the influential decision maker is more or less subtly substituted by the reality of the salesman.

It may be suspected that the columnist and his readers know in the depth of their hearts that the pleasures ordained are no longer pleasures at all, but really the duties as which they are rationalized, the rationalization containing more truth than the supposedly unconscious wish. In other words, more and more leisure time activity officially serving the purpose of fun or relaxation has actually been seized by rational self-interest and is attended not because anybody really likes it but because it is required in order to make one's way or maintain one's status. In one instance, a slip of the column gives this away: the addressee is advised to "accept all invitations" (cf. 17 November 1952, Libra; also 27 January 1953, Pisces), obviously without caring whether he likes it or not. The consummation of this trend is the obligatory participation in official "leisure time activities" in totalitarian countries.

The pleasures themselves are divided by the column into two classes, the simple ones and the unusual ones. It goes without saying that sympathy is with the simple, but sometimes the unusual ones are also encouraged, either merely for the sake of variation and "color" or possibly as a cautious means of admitting unorthodox or at least more expensive desires among the readers. What the unusual pleasures are is never hinted at: it is left up to the addressee whether to think of foreign restaurants or sex variations.

Enjoy unusual amusements and outlets.
(10 November 1952, Cancer)

The simple pleasures are again integrated within the prevailing pattern in as much as they are mainly characterized by inexpensiveness. The reader is constantly reminded that while it is all right to have some fun and to restore his balance, this should never be allowed to interfere with the well-planned budget. But the columnist's favorite pleasures are not only simple, but also "proven" (29 January 1953, Aries and Gemini) and defined as radio and television (25 January 1953, Scorpio). Gratification seems tolerable if it bears the stamp of social confirmation, if it is channelized through mass media, in other words, if it has become subject to a preconceived censorship before it even enters into the subject's experience. Thus, even in the realm where one is supposed to "let oneself go," adjustment is promoted. Pleasure itself, if admitted, has to be predigested and somehow castrated. While the column seems broad-minded enough to allow the addressee some "outlets," they have to be essentially of a spurious nature in order to obtain the blessing of the columnist. Even where the reader is authorized to get away from the routine of his life, it has to be assured that his outbreak will lead him finally into some repetition of the self-same routine he wants to get away from.

ADJUSTMENT AND INDIVIDUALITY

The nucleus of the bi-phasic approach is the maintenance of the division of work and pleasure subjecting the latter to the former's rule. However, the bi-phasic compulsion seems to expand over many other areas analogous to bureaucratic set-ups that have, as was pointed out by Max Weber, an inherent tendency to expand. This pertains particularly to the problem of adjustment to which the handling of pleasure by the column leads. While the relation between the individual and his environment is in continuous interaction with the conflict between pleasure and duty, the antagonism between the individual and the universal cannot be altogether reduced to instinctual dynamics but pertains also to the objective sociological dimension. The bi-phasic is applied to this dimension as well as to psychology in a typical pattern of advice. At times, the readers are encouraged to be strong, rugged individuals, at other times, to adjust themselves, not to be stubborn, but rather to comply with requirements from outside. The classical liberal ideas of unlimited individual activity, freedom and ruggedness are incompatible with the present developmental phase in which the individual is more and more required to obey strict organizational demands made by society. The same person can hardly be expected to be thoroughly adjusted and strongly individualistic at the same time. Yet, the individualistic ideology is maintained the more strongly, the less adequate it becomes to actual conditions. The conflicts thus induced must be taken care of by the column. It takes the individual apart as it were, into adaptive and autonomous components, thus implicitly endorsing the actual impossibility of the much praised "integration."

However, in order to get the right perspective, the underlying contradiction should not be oversimplified. In fact, the two requirements not only contradict each other, but are continuously intertwined. Thus, even today success is contingent upon individual qualities which, though utterly different from the old ones, are by no means unequivocally defined by the often stressed ego weakness[25] only but require at the same time considerable strength, namely the capacity of sacrificing oneself, as it were, for the sake of maintaining oneself. Adjustment calls for individuality. Conversely, individual qualities themselves are *a priori* measured today in terms of potential success. Thus it is taken for granted that an "original idea" is something that will "sell" and prove itself on the market.

In fact the psychological situation is rather paradoxical. He who wants to adjust himself to a competitive pattern of society or to its more hierarchical successor has to pursue his own particularistic individual interests rather ruthlessly in order to find recognition – he has, so to speak, to adjust through non-adjustment, through unwavering emphasis on his limited self-interests and their concomitant psychological limitations. Conversely the development of spontaneous individuality implies by necessity some degree of adjustment. Henri Bergson has pointed out in his *Laughter*,[26] that the psychological calcifications which make an individual comical in an esthetic sense indicate some failure in his maturity and are bound up with his incapacity to cope with changing social situations, going as far as stating that, in a way, the concept of "character" denoting a rigidified personality pattern impervious to life experience is comical *per se*. Thus, the emphasis on individuality *in abstracto*, its severance from contacts with the outside world results in a way in its maladjustment. It induces compulsive behavior which we are tempted usually to attribute only to the opposite, to the pressure of an alienated and conventionalized reality. It is therefore dangerous, though

78

easily understandable, in a social set-up in which a fetish is made of the concept of adjustment to isolate the concepts of individuality and adjustment and to play up undialectically one against the other. It is this complex structure which provides the column with the opportunity to somehow find a common denominator for the contradictory requirements of being a personality and being, as it is called euphemistically, "co-operative." The fact that one of the contradictory requirements often fulfills the other unwittingly is skillfully exploited.

The encouragement of direct adjustment to outside forces often takes the form of glorifying, to use once again the terminology of popular psychology, the extrovert at the expense of the introvert.[27] It often seems that the column really does not expect an integration of social norms with the personality but rather wants the addressees to obey requirements from outside to the extent to which it has to be done while at the same time being led to ruthlessly falling back on a kind of anarchic ruggedness as soon as they can get away with it – the configuration of rigid obedience and lack of true introjection of norms being itself a symptom of something wrong underneath. People are continuously reminded that they should not brood, but should seize their opportunity when it is time to act, that they should be "pleasant" to others, avoid quarreling and be "sensible."

> ... be very considerate at home where tension mounts if you display nervousness.
> (19 November 1952, Taurus)
> ... control desire to let fly with choice sarcastic comments.
> (21 November 1952, Capricorn)
> Replace mulling over troubles by new interests.
> (9 December 1952, Pisces)
> Temptation to bawl out co-workers should be sternly repressed.
> (9 December 1952, Cancer)
> Be considerate of others. Work all questions out in cooperative fashion.
> (13 December 1952, Scorpio)
> A.M. brings many problems into open to test your self-control.
> (30 November 1952, Aries)
> You really are explosive during morning without any apparent reason. It's just the planets testing your self-control. Keep calm.
> (31 December 1952, Cancer)
> ... be more social.
> (12 November 1952, Virgo)

Get out of yourself; make every new association possible.
    (13 November 1952, Aquarius)
Much pleasure is yours by keeping around happy, cheerful personalities.
    (14 December 1952, Cancer)
Much happiness is easily yours now if you accept invitations. . .
    (12 January 1953, Leo)
Attach yourself to all about you who are vital, dynamic and able to advance you quickly.
    (13 January 1953, Virgo)
... Get out in the world; meet all those who can show you more modern ways.
    (20 January 1953, Scorpio)
You are eager to get those plans into execution. Fine. Lose no time; contact all friends able to help; expand into new outlets in all directions.
    (3 January 1953, Sagittarius)
... contact all possible and forcefully state your own desired aims in a charming manner. Discuss the future with practical friends. Act!
    (January 9 1953, Pisces)
Action!
    (January 18 1953, Scorpio)

Most of these devices express an awareness of some difficulties on the part of the addressee. Thus precisely the kind of compulsive and isolated elderly women who must provide a good part of the astrological audience are often afraid of any new contact, if not of any contacts at all. The column somehow comes to their aid. "Psychotic characters," in spite of their overrealistic defenses and success in isolating their delusions, are still continuously threatened by the loss of any relationship to reality and it is one of the aims of the column, inasmuch as it tries to "help," to maintain this relationship on a superficial level. Similar experiences stand behind other advices on the same dimension. "Being pleasant" refers to the petty quarrels particularly characteristic of crankish women from the lower middle classes, "not brooding" to the psychological habit of "ruminating" to be found in obsessive-compulsive persons. While the column strengthens their neurotic attitudes in certain directions, it tries to channelize them or to isolate them from their everyday functioning, to remove overt symptoms which might hinder the reader's efficiency.

One specific advice promoting "extroverted" adjustment is the attack on the "inflated ego." Reckoning with the narcissistic[28] sensitivities of the addressee, the columnist is careful not to blame him for such a deformity, but rather refers to threatening higher-ups and officials in such terms. However, it may safely be assumed that the underlying idea is to warn the addressee himself against having such unrealistic ideas about his own person.

> You feel dynamic, determined to put your plans in effect at all costs. However, do so cleverly without alienating others with big ego who resent other's success.
> (14 December 1952, Scorpio)
> An executive or a government official with an inflated ego is likely to put a monkey wrench in your plans.
> (29 January 1953, Leo)

So far as the higher-ups are concerned, the device attempts by reference to the "inflated ego" to mitigate the unpleasant impact of hierarchical relationships. It is the higher-up, not the little man, who somehow appears unbalanced. His show of strength is presented as a symptom of inherent weakness in order to make it easier for the inferior to obey by suggesting that he is actually the stronger. The trivial psychological insight that pretentiousness is frequently a mere reaction formation to the popular inferiority complex is utilized in order to make it easier for the addressee to cope with his own social dependence. The idolized extrovert does not overassert himself, but rather accepts what the world thinks of him as the ultimate yardstick for his evaluation. Defamation of the "inflated ego" is all-pervasive in popular psychological literature, including the works of the late Miss Horney such as *The Neurotic Personality of our Time* or *New Ways in Psychoanalysis*.[29] Feeding upon reminiscences of the old psychiatric concept of delusions of grandeur, this stereotype comes pretty close to the idea expressed in nicknames such as "*Cafe Grössenwahn*": that the introvert, the retiring person is unjustifiedly haughty and that his withdrawal from the triviality and brutality of everyday life is actually indicative of weakness only and of a distorted picture of reality. The grain of truth contained in such notions is abused for conformist purposes. The world is right; the outsider wrong. Thus, as well as by the closely related pattern of anti-intellectualism, general leveling is promoted. According to this ideology nobody really should believe in himself and his intrinsic qualities, but should prove his mettle by functioning within a given set-up as well as the others do.

According to the bi-phasic technique, however, at other times the readers are encouraged to be "individual." But here something analogous to the treatment of pleasure can be observed, somehow leading to the suspicion that individuality itself is regarded as a kind of luxury which some people sometimes can afford and which has to be exalted as "a cultural good," but which should never seriously interfere with the smooth running of the social machinery.

Looking more closely at the individual qualities advocated by the column, we will discover that it practically never refers to the mature, experienced character defined by power of resistance against external pressure, never to a specific and strongly developed ego. Rather the supposedly positive aspects of individuality are isolated traits severed from the ego development – in fact, just the opposite of the ego, namely irrational gifts with a dash of the magical. The difficulty of stressing individuality in persons whose ego is assumed to be weak is overcome by substituting individuality with rudimentary archaic qualities which may be regarded as the "possession" of the individual independent of his ego formation. Just in as much as such qualities have little to do with the ego and his rationality, they are treated as though they were "unique" and individualized in an absolute sense. When the column appeals to the addressee's individuality, it mentions almost invariably blessings such as "charm," "personal magnetism,"

> ... keep steadfast in impressing higher-up with your innate abilities.
> (10 November 1952, Aquarius)
> ... improving your outlets and personal charm, unusually effective.
> (12 November 1952, Taurus)
> ... keep cheerful, exuding magnetism.
> (14 November 1952, Aquarius)
> Your own personal charm enhanced by supplies available.
> (13 November 1952, Libra)
> ... improve personal charm.
> (17 November 1952, Sagittarius)
> ... every ounce of your magnetic charm is more evident.
> (18 November 1952, Leo)
> ... bring out your magnetic charm.
> (19 November 1952, Aries)
> Exude magnetism.
> (21 November 1952, Libra)
> Exude charm.
> (17 November 1952, Aries)

or even their "own intuition:"

... flash inspiration of brilliance shows method for improving joint undertaking.

(10 November 1952, Sagittarius)

Use that fine mind in A.M. to bring into expression more workable plans in all departments of your affairs.

(16 November 1952, Virgo)

Then your intuitions give you correct answers during afternoon.

(16 November 1952, Scorpio)

Get that clever mind of yours busy early mapping big day to advance by threshing out. . .

(20 November 1952, Scorpio)

the emphasis on irrational intuitiveness set against rational thinking being extremely popular in a rationalized world.[30] It seems that the individualistic categories here involved are treated as what has come to be known in economics as "natural monopolies." Thus they are characteristically called "assets," subject to the measuring rod of success, of practicality, just as pleasure has been treated as a subfunction of work. If the individual lives up to the expectations of the column, he develops, stresses and shows off these qualities which he shares with no one else because their "rarity" gives them a sales value. Being different, thus, is integrated into the pattern of universal sameness as an object of barter. Individuality itself is submerged in the process of transformation of ends into means. The reader is incessantly encouraged to impress others with his individuality by making use of those "assets" which seem to be so highly coveted that everybody is prepared to attribute them to himself if he is given a chance to do so.

Even this is not a wild and unrealistic construction on the part of the column, but reflects something that has been observed long ago. Aldous Huxley has described in one of his early novels a person who can switch his charm on and off at will. This seems to be by no means a unique experience. When people learn, in a competitive world, that certain manifestations, originally quite involuntary and irrational, such as a smile or a particular tone of voice, impress people in a favorable way, they actually learn to convert such expressive qualities into an "asset" and to display "that famous grin" at every befitting occasion.

While the advice to be practical coincides with the idea of being realistic and in many respects actually amounts to realism, the underlying irrational mechanisms of compulsion manifest themselves in certain traits of the fostered sense of the practical which are irrational themselves and give a picture of what might be called a lack of sense of proportion, sometimes indicative of serious psychological deformities. These deformities usually follow the all-pervasive pattern of substituting ends for means. What it dubbed practical, sometimes assumes the weight of an "*überwertige Idee*" (an idea that plays in a person's stream of consciousness a disproportionate role determined by psychological factors). Viewed from reality, actions and attitudes are heavily emphasized of which effect and importance is actually of an extremely limited scope.

Thus advice, innocuous but trite, of taking care of one's appearance plays a surprisingly large role in the column.

Also improve personal appearance.
    (12 November 1952, Virgo)
Rather, get your personal appearance, health in better shape.
    (12 December 1952, Aquarius)
More charm to self, improvement to car, etc. possible by taking approved methods for "face-lifting" treatments.
    (13 November 1952, Gemini)
Your own day to take those beauty treatments, get haircuts, do whatever increases your personal charm and sense of wellbeing.
    (13 November 1952, Libra)
... get personal appearance improved to bring out your magnetic charm.
    (19 November 1952, Aries)
... YOUR personal appearance must be impeccable.
    (22 November 1952, Taurus)

Incessant stress suggests the exaltation of cleanliness and health to the level of ideals, a well-known trait of the anal syndrome. The psychotic symptom of paying extreme attention to the patient's own body which somehow seems to be alienated from "himself" is also pertinent. Cranks fall as easily for astrology as for health food movements, natural healing and similar panaceas. The sociological value of cleanliness is tied up with the cultural heritage of puritanism, a fusion of the ideal of sexual purity with that of a neat body – *mens sana in corpore sano*. At the back of this is the repression of the sense of smelling.

All these irrational propensities are championed by the column's pseudo-rational pattern of externalization. What matters is what one looks like and not what one is; the means-for-ends idea has done away with the last vestige of anything existing for its own sake.

Closely related is the frequent advice to "arrange property matters or discuss finances with the family." They are above all indicators of the anal cathexis to tangible, fixed property, as it is represented to the addressee, mainly in the sphere of his private life since probably only a minority of the addressees own any business. But apart from these well-known psychological features some specific sociological considerations also enter the picture. The possibility of acquiring money and property, or even the chance of making a start for it, is much more limited for most people today than it was rightly or wrongly supposed to be during the heyday of classical liberalism. Yet the Horatio Alger myth is continuously upheld as one of the most important stimuli that induce people's efforts. Here again, the column looks for a way out. If one cannot gain property as of old, it is suggestively implied that by clever disposition of what one has, by planning and scheduling in a manner appealing anyway to compulsive persons, the same success may be achieved that is now denied to expansive business enterprise. Making charts, timetables, schedules, and similar formalistic ventures serve as substitutes for the actual money making. This is why the idea of budgeting, making plans and similar symptoms of unrealistic realism are favored by the column. It is as though the imaginary vice-president, since he is no vice-president after all, should at least playfully fulfill the latter's function, a device which by the way is also sometimes supplied in business education where office boys have to act symbolically as executives for one day.

> You have imagination, vision which you can reduce to exact expression – find out how others invest, increase income; then apply to your own responsibilities; pay bills.
> (13 November 1952, Pisces)
> Look to new methods to add to present income, lop off unnecessary expenses; getting in huddle with serious workers brings new aspect to your present obligations.
> (18 November 1952, Scorpio)
> ... devise new avenues for making money.
> (19 November 1952, Scorpio)
> ... arrange improved methods for securing more income, happiness by cooperative measures.
> (20 November 1952, Gemini)
> Work all angles that bring you added money, possessions, good things of life.
> (22 November 1952, Capricorn)

Yet the old concept of unbridled acquisitiveness is so deeply embedded in a business culture that it cannot be discarded or entirely repressed by spurious pseudo-activity though the columnist is well aware that it is no longer adequate to present-day economy. Here the columnist finds a rather ingenious way out, falling back to astrology's otherwise concealed basis of superstition. There are quite a few hints of substantial material gains, but they are rarely if ever attributed to the reader's own work or to business profits, but almost always to highly improbable and irrational providential acts of fate.

> Unexpected help from hidden source makes all property conditions easier to solve.
> (23 November 1952, Aries)
> Persons, messages, calls from distance bring element of good fortune toward securing determined wish.
> (26 November 1952, Aries)
> Noon finds unexpected support secretly given you.
> (6 December 1952, Virgo)
> Unexpected benefits are probable but whatever you force through yourself will boomerang.
> (20 January 1953, Aries)

Through taking recourse to the simple technique of the fortune teller and discarding the column's usual reserve, the reader is assured that at some particular time pecuniary affluence will be heaped upon him if he is born under a particular sign of the day, or by using mysterious "friends" as the agents who bestow fabulous benefactions upon him. He is neither expected to believe that he could earn it nor to accept that he can never have it. Thus he is spoken to and given unreasonable promises like a child. Obviously the columnist figures out that the reader's wishes in this direction are so strong that he can get away with even such unreasonable promises on account of the momentary gratifications they provide though the reader knows in the depth of his heart that the promise will never be fulfilled. At this point the column profits from the same mentality which draws people to gambling, horse betting and similar devices for making easy money. Propensity for irrational material gain seems to be contingent upon the shrinking chances of making big money as a pioneer or on a rational basis of calculation.

Sometimes the wild promises made by the column take the form of referring to the addressee's "fondest" hopes or "deepest" desires.

> Discuss your fondest hopes with relatives.
> (27 January, Taurus)

Such references are "blanks" which can and probably will be filled in by each adept of the column according to his specific emotional requirements. Just because his "fondest hopes" are concerned, he is temporarily prepared to accept the most improbable promises. What appears to be simply a linguistic mannerism of the column reveals itself in its over-all context as a very clever device to catch the addressee. It may also be that the rather abstract form "your fondest hopes" is one of the ways in which real, uncensored instinctual urges of the addressees are sanctioned by the columnist without the possibility of his being put on the spot and having to take the responsibility for anything he might have said.

While nursing hopes for considerable gains outside of the limitation of normal business processes, "a stroke of luck," the column is not satisfied with entirely irrational promises. Sometimes the addressee is, though utterly cautiously and indirectly, encouraged not simply to rely on his luck, but, to borrow the phrase of Lessing's Riccaut de la Marlinière,[31] to "*corriger la fortune.*" The form in which this idea crops up is the use of expressions such as "behind scenes activities" reference to which is often made in a positive sense.

Behind-scenes huddle with personal expert with finances shows way to *increase* your assets.
   (17 November 1952, Sagittarius)
A.M. finds need for secret huddle with member of family to eliminate present worry.
   (19 November 1952, Virgo)
... plan future secretly.
   (21 November 1952, Capricorn)
... make quiet arrangements.
   (21 November 1952, Aquarius)
This is your day to manipulate matters cleverly behind the scenes to improve your happiness.
   (3 January 1953, Leo)
Much behind-the-scenes discussion can show intelligent ways to increase your revenue.
   (9 January 1953, Aquarius)
Behind-scenes activity to devise a better system for performing irksome chores will bring more contentment at home as well.
   (13 January 1953, Aquarius)

Apart from the constant advice "to strike a bargain," to "improve property" and "make schedules," the columnist fosters the idea that the addressee can get ahead in the business hierarchy only by finagling himself, by use of personal connections and sly diplomacy rather than by strict working activities. This has some rather evil implications. Within the pattern of modern mass delusions, the idea of conspiracies is always present – an idea doubtlessly of a projective nature. Encouraging "behind-the-scenes" activities is an inconspicuous form of conjuring up such tendencies usually projected upon outgroups. Those who persistently blame others for indulging in conspiracies have a strong tendency to engage in plots themselves and this is taken up and reproduced in the column. In view of the somewhat risky character of this admonition, the bi-phasic approach here proves especially valuable to the column. The advice to finagle is countered – undone in the psychoanalytic sense – by interspersed reminders to be law-abiding and always to keep within the realm of the permissible, an advice that chimes in with the column's outward attitude of over-all conventionality and conformity.

> Strict adherence to the spirit as well as the letter of the law greatly please harassed higher-up.
> (14 November 1952, Capricorn)

But morality too appears externalized: one has to account for one's actions to others, to wit, the higher-up, rather than to oneself. At the same time, the idea of accounting is not so much presented as a normal duty in business as it is pictured as a threat. The addressee is advised to behave in such a way that, when and if accounting comes, he will be spared by the thunderstorm with the undertone that by keeping his books either pedantically or cleverly things will blow over.

> Use utmost care in handling funds involving others.
> (10 November 1952, Gemini)
> ... see that every item of worldly affairs is exactly right so no criticism comes to you.
> (17 November 1952, Pisces)
> Credit interests require more than usual care to prevent unintentional error that causes higher-up to look askance at your abilities; P.M. systematize joint concerns.
> (18 November 1952, Pisces)
> ... be sure you account exactly bank, tax, property obligations.
> (22 November 1952, Aries)
> ... arrange joint funds exactly.
> (6 December 1952, Taurus)
> Your disinclination toward making present associations more lucrative necessitates careful approach to authority who would flare up unless exact picture is given.
> (3 January 1953, Pisces)

Take no chances with credit and career! When others demand accounting from you for present obligations, be grateful and give meticulous explanations.

(8 January 1953, Capricorn)

An authority will demand an accounting if you take any chances.

(14 January 1953, Capricorn)

The A.M. requires exactness in all matters connected with those in authority.

(15 January 1953, Aries)

Your financial problems show need for more systematizing and wisdom in handling.

(21 January 1953, Pisces)

While the column implicitly seems to agree to the very widespread, though unofficial ideology that everything is permitted as long as one is not caught, the periodical reminder to readers to remain within the limits of the law is also indicative of the fact that the columnist presupposes very strong inclinations for law-breaking and anarchy in his readers which are the reverse of that social integration and rigid conformity overtly upheld. Everpresent destructive urges are ready to smash the very same control mechanism by which they are engendered.

Carefully double check all your accounts, statements and joint obligations. That temptation to forsake duty for pleasure is not good.

(21 January 1953, Gemini)

Use utmost care in handling funds involving others; postpone expensive pleasures until more propitious time; your security improves by finishing present obligations.

(10 November 1952, Gemini)

One final irrational aspect of the idea of "being practical" emerging in the column may be mentioned. It is the idea that "your family background" will indicate to the addressee the right way.

Your inherited background gives answers for right attitude to assume toward higher-ups who question your ability, viewpoint.

(23 November 1952, Capricorn)

Inherited, family principles are to your advantage in A.M.

(7 December 1952, Cancer)

Your family background provides answer to your deepest needs at moment.

(14 December 1952, Libra)

Your background provides correct answer to A.M. preoccupations, glumness.
(21 December 1952, Capricorn)
The solid principles of your background conflict with your desire
for risky, adventurous pleasures; stick to your proven outlets.
(11 January 1953, Scorpio)
In the A.M. your family background points the way to your
advance in all directions.
(18 January 1953, Aries)
Peace of mind today is attained through attention to practical
problems and proven principles from your family background.
(25 January 1953, Virgo)

This idea again is close to others being dealt with in this study, such as
the treatment of personal qualities as natural monopolies or the bi-phasic
idea of being modern and being conservative, the family background, of
course, belonging to the conservative side.

But above all, this device is another attempt to cope with the
threatening disappearance of free competitive activity. The notion of
those who "belong" plays an increasing role sociologically linked to
"closed societies" and particularly observable in totalitarian countries.
Conjuring up the "family background" may possibly be an appeal to
those who, being native, white, gentile Americans and whose families
have lived in the States a long time may fancy themselves as the "right
people" and expect certain privileges. The "family background" is
supposed to function as reassuring narcissistically and also realistically in
as far as people with such a background might be admitted more easily to
influential positions. Behind the family background lurks the idea of
numerus clausus. But the range of the device is by no means limited to the
happy few, but the majority is treated as a privileged group in order to
counteract feelings of atomization and personal insecurity as part of the
technique of modern mass manipulation pointed out by Karl Mannheim
in his book *Man and Society*.[32]

In the column of 21 December those born under the sign of
Capricorn are reassured that their background provides "correct answer
to preoccupations, glumness." On the surface this means that they can
draw on their traditions in order to solve their problems – certainly not
a very convincing promise. The real psychological message is rather
"Think about the marvelous family you come from and you will feel
elated and superior to those on whom you depend and who might have
annoyed you." It may be mentioned that a highly prejudiced subject

studied in the *Authoritarian Personality*[33] remarked: "All my friends are from marvelous families."

Imaginativeness is often referred to. Here, however, something shows up that is indicative of subtle psychological changes reflecting rather drastic social ones. The old idea that money can only be made through originality and new ideas and that success on the market depends not only on meeting demands by offers, but in either creating new demands or in offering something better and cheaper than what is at the moment available, is still maintained. But the column must acknowledge that the opportunities for the implementation of innovations and original ideas are extremely limited today for most persons. Thus, again cleverly relying on compulsive patterns, the emphasis on imaginativeness is presented mostly in terms of business administration and business organization. While, of course, the opportunities for really essential changes on this level are also severely restricted, they still seem to be more in line with the over-all organization of professional life within which people find themselves caught than the idea of an inventiveness which presupposes a much more individualistic set-up. Thus, the addressees are encouraged to make changes within the given organizatory framework, by necessity more or less routine provisions, which we may assume fall within the very narrow range of their influence or their knowledge and which have presumably little influence upon the real course of events. The concept of originality seems to have shrunk to the ideal of each person's becoming an efficiency expert in his own circumscribed realm.

... you can replace by adopting unthought, untried new plan. Be open-minded.
(10 November 1952, Scorpio)
You have imagination, vision which you can reduce to exact expression – find out how others invest, increase income; then apply to your own responsibilities; pay bills.
(13 November 1952, Pisces)
... your creative ideas are fine, attend to investments, too.
(15 November 1952, Gemini)
Creative expressions unusually appealing so use your sense of neat touch, the artistic, to attain more success.
(22 November 1952, Libra)

Modifications such as that of the concept of originality, indicate that the worldly wisdom that steers the column is by no means limited to popular psychology, but includes also economics, as might be expected of an approach dedicated to the very sphere where psychological and rational motivations are fused. Some of the "spread out" contradictory advice testifies to economic problems of old standing. Here belongs, above all, the alternative advice to be "modern" and to be "conservative," related to but not identical with the dimension of being "imaginative" and being "sensible." Again both terms are introduced mostly with reference to business methods, techniques and improvements. Again individuality is involved. Only he who thinks by himself and offers something new is supposed to make good. On the other hand, it is traditionally accepted that those who have dared to make innovations but had only limited financial resources run the risk of being wiped out by financially stronger interests even if they think of some real novelty: the image of the starving inventor is well-known. Under present conditions the slogan "be modern" is apt to deteriorate into a mere sham. Real technological advancement is left to technological experts frequently far removed from the business set-up whereas he who wants to make headway in a large-scale business organization has generally to be "conservative" not so much perhaps, nowadays, for fear of bankruptcy, but for fear that as an employee one would appear as a crank, transgressing the place in the hierarchy if he continuously made or advocated innovations. While the column attempts to solve this impasse by simply demanding that the reader sometimes be "conservative," sometimes "modern," the real difficulty is dodged. Both advices which have their full meaning in the sphere of production only are transferred to the sphere of consumption which still gives the individual at least the illusion of a certain freedom of choice between what is advertised as excitingly modern and as cozily and quaintly old-fashioned. Even more often the term conservative is used in the loose meaning of pursuing a "conservative" financial policy, i.e., carefully avoiding unnecessary spending: frequently high-sounding statements of the column amount in practice to the recommendation of thriftiness. When the column advises the reader to be modern it seems almost imperative that he should buy modern equipment particularly for his home – an advice affiliated with gadgeteering. When he is advised to be conservative, it means that he should keep his expenditures under control. The relegation of the change between the modern and the conservative to the sphere of consumption, however, points itself to a somewhat self-contradictory situation. While the present huge offer of goods calls for modern-minded people prepared to buy any novelty, the buyer's mentality thus built up destroys reserves, threatens those to whom buying becomes a compulsion and is often presented as though it would potentially endanger the whole economic structure by undermining buying capacity itself. In order to make it right, as a real conformist, to everyone, the column has to promote sales and sales resistance, an ungrateful task to be mastered only by again spreading the advice over different periods of time.

Your own ideas need revitalizing to keep up with present worldly conditions; fine for studying modern systems; a progressive associate helps greatly if asked.
(16 November 1952, Capricorn)
Your associates all seem to be at sixes and sevens, nothing seems to make sense. Stick to tried, proven principles, then all goes along very smoothly.
(4 December 1952, Aries)
Nothing seems easy to do, you can't find right articles of goods, foods, or other supplies. Be very conservative. Then you avoid mistakes that others, unaware it is a difficult day, are making.
(4 December 1952, Leo)
Adopting more up-to-date attitude brings you protection.
(9 December 1952, Scorpio)
... use much care in all property matters, joint ventures; your hunches are poor.
(6 January 1953, Pisces)

The term "modern," as used by this column, is frequently the equivalent of "scientific:"
Forget past, worn-out systems, interests; look to modern trends in educational and scientific fields vital to your needs.
(5 January 1953, Capricorn)
Getting down to brass tacks in an up-to-date scientific manner improving your outlets and personal charm unusually effective.
(12 November 1952, Taurus)
This is your day to get out from your conservative, conventional outlets; see how rest of world lives, take to yourself modern methods that improve your efficiency.
(12 November 1952, Capricorn)
Some of our long-standing views need to be brought up-to-date for present workableness.
(16 November 1952, Aries)
Adopting more modern spiritual, educational, scientific principles gives more happiness, success in creative interests.
(23 November 1952, Gemini)

This involves the idea that one *saves* money by introducing innovations rather than running any risk. At the same time the admonition to be "scientific" airs a peculiar concern of the column. Astrology, and occultism as a whole, has as indicated before a strong urge to overcome suspicions of magical practices in a rationalized business culture. Science is the bad conscience of occultism and the more irrational the justification of its pretenses, the more it is stressed that there is nothing phony about it. While the column avoids controversies on the merits of astrology, but for good psychological reasons takes its authority for granted, it indirectly follows this urge by its studious bows to science in general.[34]

Viewed psychoanalytically, the interpretation of astrological ambition to present an apocryphal cult as scientific in order to assuage a bad conscience probably does not go deep enough. The ideal of security, the conquest of anxiety, seems to be involved. There exists a compulsive fear of committing an error and, as a correlate, a high gratification in being "absolutely right" even if irreproachability may be obtained only by complete triviality and meaninglessness – a philosophy reminiscent of the pedantry of the anal character. The more dubious the statements craved for, the stronger the need for this type of protection. On top of early fixations, this attitude is reinforced in the Oedipal phase[35] by the fear of the father who discourages sexual curiosity and teaches the child that it is too stupid to understand and should confine itself to what is conventionally done and known rather than embark on any exploratory ventures – an attitude reflected by the column in as much as it always refers to fixed unalterable necessities and never goes beyond what is made to appear as "positive." The reader of the column is always supposed to act according to prescriptions. The feeling that nothing can happen after withdrawal from sexual longing, related to castration fear,[36] replaces the enjoyment originally longed for: security itself may become a sexual substitute. Yet the irrationality of this displacement is never lost sight of entirely. This is mirrored rather exactly in viewing astrology as a science which promises absolute and unchallengable security (mainly because it cannot be put to the test) while the ultimate source of the security – the threat – is hidden and utterly unrecognizable. The hints of impending danger may be the last of heavily censored traces of castration fear. Certainly among the truly unconscious messages of the column, one of the most effective should read "safety first," a slogan which itself is to be regarded, apart from its rational merits, as a psychological hieroglyph.

RUGGEDNESS AND DEPENDENCE

Closely related to the contradiction between adjustment and

individuality is that between dependence and ruggedness. Viewed psychologically, the actual weakness of the individual in the social set-up is concomitant with serious narcissistic losses which have somehow to be made up vicariously by the column. For the purpose, it draws again on some phenomena of reality. The psychological feeling of dependence seems to be on the increase. But giving up one's individuality requires the same effort and investment of libido formerly needed in order to develop individuality – in a way, the same "ruggedness." Thus the column's task is twofold – in as much as the situation makes for subordination, it has to reassure its readers that they are nevertheless rugged individuals; in as much as the situation calls for real ruggedness, it has to assuage their own feeling of impotence. As to "aggressiveness," it obviously goes with the ideal of being practical; as to subordination, this seems to be related to conscience and generally to a timid and withdrawn personality structure. A common denominator is sought for both types.

It can easily be seen that the dimension here considered does by no means coincide with those previously stated. No mechanical parallelism between the three main dichotomies analyzed by our study would be adequate. Since the total approach of the column is, as may have crystallized by now, a definite pattern, a structural unit, everything is somehow connected with everything else, and the analytic isolation of various factors has always something of the arbitrary. Yet the isolating operations we have carried through are invited by the nature of the material. The column's model of ruggedness has very little in common with those irrational qualities of the individual it stresses otherwise; and the sense of obedience it promotes is equally distant from the salesman traits of the happy extrovert. The antagonism here under discussion expresses itself frequently in the habit of sometimes advising people to be definite, sometimes to think carefully before they act. The warning not to hesitate[37] is probably derived from the pressure of time under which most people have to work together with the impact of the widespread, culturally conditioned taboo of "armchair thinking." Yet today it is dangerous to practically anyone to act upon his own responsibility. People who make supposedly wrong decisions are rarely in a position to follow up these decisions independently, to make them good or to take subsequent actions by which the previous ones may be justified, but are generally called on the carpet if the decision does not agree with the policy set by higher agencies. This structural change typically involved in the bureaucratization of modern society, is met by the column's advice not to act hastily and irrevocably, particularly not to be led by impulse into actions, but rather to think carefully and particularly to discuss problems with others before acting.

> ... discuss thoroughly with those familiar with true facts, operating principles.
> (25 November 1952, Cancer)

> You see both sides of every question confronting you. You are able to convince all colleagues of your stand.
> (25 November 1952, Capricorn)

> You feel dynamic, determined to put your plans in effect at all costs. However do so cleverly without alienating others with big ego who resent other's success.
> (14 December 1952, Scorpio)

> Be careful that in haste to do chore and get to church or off on trip you do not damage articles of clothing. In P.M. confer with associate about new big venture.
> (4 January 1953, Libra)

> Your determination to spend much on investments and pleasures is all right, but not now; await a better moment for this step – watch these suggestions.
> (7 January 1953, Gemini)

Concomitantly the general tendency of the column to prepare the addressees to act as members of "teams" comes to the fore. It is as though it had been accepted as a major ideological tenet that everything can be settled by majority decisions taken at some "meeting," a caricature of democracy. At the same time, the continuous encouragement to talk things over with others appeals to the conviction of many people mentioned previously, that others know more about them and their own difficulties than they know themselves – an all-pervasive sense of self-alienation. It is in this connection that the concept of "understanding" crops up in the column. Sociologically the stress on understanding, being understood as well as understanding others, probably reflects social atomization, the reverse and concomitant of collectivization as studied by David Riesman in his *Lonely Crowd*.[38] The column calculates, probably correctly, that whoever is subject to cold, dehumanized, rigid and alienated social relationships feels insufficiently understood. Objective estrangement is made up suggestively, synthetically, as it were, by ubiquitous "human interest." Thus continuous advice is given to seek other persons who understand one and to try to understand others.

Make sure you are most understanding with members of family

who are distraught.
(22 November 1952, Scorpio)
Be most careful with all in authority. Be understanding that they
have problems.
(18 December 1952, Aries)
Bombastic associate, enemy unable to find personal peace of mind
tries to take you also deep into doldrums. Be understanding but
don't fall for this dreary line.
(30 December 1952, Capricorn)
Your personal resentments keep desired – and desirable favors from
you; so smile, see other fellow's view, be kind to officials, then,
P.M. bring much happiness.
(23 January 1953, Capricorn)

The latter advice is sometimes administered under the viewpoint that
one is able to overcome one's own difficulties by identifying oneself with
someone even worse off. Thus even humaneness is treated as a means
rather than an end. It is as though finally the sphere of the internal itself
were to be incorporated into the range of externalization by manipulating the active and passive phases of understanding. Inwardness is
integrated into the machinery.

While this can be partly explained by the tendency to transform
objective problems into subjective and psychological ones, it also means
that one should be prepared to give in to the supposedly higher wisdom
of those whom one has to obey anyway. Psychological self-reflection is
transformed into a tool furthering adjustment. Meekness towards the
more powerful seems to do less damage to so-called self-esteem if
cloaked as the outcome of higher insight either into oneself or into those
whom one obeys.

Not infrequently the bi-phasic admonition appears actually in
behavioral terms. Sometimes the addressee as a successful business man
has to be "dynamic" sometimes he has to "give in." It seems, however,
that the advice to be strong and rugged is meted out rather reluctantly.
While the veneer of the addressee's independence is guarded, he is
advised most of the time to be strong only with people weaker or at least
on an equal footing with him, particularly with his family, but also
occasionally with the "friends" whose function throughout the column
is somewhat ambivalent. On the whole the column takes the idea of
"ruggedness" less seriously than its counterpart.

The idea of "giving in" is usually cloaked in such a way that all
potentially unpleasant demands to be expected from the outside are

presented as though they were well-meaning advice from other people. Here again, adjustment necessitated by stronger conditions is mitigated as an achievement of insight. The soft-pedalling is most of the time brought about by the device of personalization. The requirements of reality are constantly reduced to the human figures who might want or order something. These persons rather than the requirements themselves are continuously characterized. Generally they are well-meaning, experienced, friendly, but at the same time, powerful and somehow authority figures; sometimes, however, provision is made for negative experiences with them.

These negative characteristics are generally stated in a way calling for pity with the strong rather than for their rejection. If it is envisaged that the addressee is being hurt by someone, he is made to understand that he is not to hit back but rather to assume an attitude indicative of his own inner superiority and to yield. The psychiatrically well-known pattern of "identification with the aggressor"[39] seems to be one of the column's basic positive ideas on human relationships. Perhaps it can be seen nowhere more clearly than here how the column, and the popular psychology to which it is related, strengthens defenses rather than dissolves them. Human relationships are viewed in an authoritarian way, organized according to an implicit hierarchy of the strong and the weak, and, accordingly, almost entirely on the ruggedness vs. dependence level.

CATEGORIES OF HUMAN RELATIONSHIPS

We conclude our analysis of the typical ideas and techniques of the column by mentioning a few of the most important categories of human relations as conceived by the column.

Family and neighbors

The column's attitude towards the *family* is largely one of conventional, official optimism which does not admit that anything might be wrong with the addressee's closest in-group. To be sure, there are tensions but it is assumed that basically everything is love and harmony. One might say that the true problems of the family are brought out only negatively, namely by an almost complete neglect of the internalized, affective aspects of family life – here everything is extroverted, too, and the family is viewed either as a resource of help and comfort

... support comes from member of family to lighten present burdens.

(10 November 1952, Leo)

or as a source of complaints and demands which one has to satisfy to a certain extent in order to have a tolerable life. Thus, certainly unconsciously, a picture of coldness is obtained due to the lack of anything like empathy with the others. The family is relegated to leisure time; in the bi-phasic organization of the column it is mentioned almost exclusively with reference to P.M., in the same sphere in which the addressee is advised to fix his home or to go out.

In certain situations, the addressee is advised to give in to the family. Typical is the assumption that he might be inclined to spend beyond his means – possibly for pleasures such as alcohol and gambling. Since the wife is the one who, in the last analysis, has to manage with the budget, the addressee is being taught to talk over financial matters with her although she is rarely referred to as such but mainly in the more abstract term "the family," perhaps in order not to make him feel henpecked. In this pattern, the family functions as the agent of social control of the addressee's instinctual urges. Following the same line, the caution of the wife, in talking over business matters, is sometimes supposed to prevent the husband from rebelling in his professional life and thus to endanger his job. Such bits of common sense are never stated in so many words, but in rather abstract terms allowing for various interpretations. Thus, the talking over of finances with the family might also serve the opposite purpose, namely of controlling the purse strings against the wife's inclination towards heavy spending. Here the wife, as "consumer," is regarded as more irrational than the husband as "provider." Such apparent inconsistencies express fairly well the complexities of actual life situations. Anyway, the prevailing idea is that the family still is the only "team" knitted together by so strong common interests that one can rely on each other with little reservations and somehow make joint plans in order to cope successfully with a threatening and potentially hostile world. The family is constructed as a kind of protective organization built exclusively on the principle of give and take rather than as a spontaneous form of living together. This may well reflect certain structural changes in the modern family.[40]

Therefore, the addressee has to "calculate" very carefully his relationships with his family. He has to pay for the help and solidarity he expects. There is the ever-present threat of nagging and it is this point where the column tends to emphasize the "giving in," by a cautious

THE STARS DOWN TO EARTH

soft-pedalled behavior and continuous consideration of what might invite the family's wrath. In this respect the family often appears as a kind of threatening archaic clan whose verdicts prevail over the dependent subject. Behind the idea of nagging there is the correct expectation that the division between the spheres of production and consumption, of work and leisure, never runs smoothly. The fact that life itself tends to become increasingly a mere appendix to the business that should serve life needs involves an absurdity with which even the supposedly well-adjusted cannot possibly get away without conflict. The wife's nagging is, without her being aware of it, a protest against a situation often aggravated because the man who has to control himself during the working hours and to repress his aggressions is prone to let them loose against those who are close to him, but have less power than himself. The worldly wisdom of the column is quite aware of all this as well as the fact that in such conflicts women are usually more naive than men and that the appeal to the latter's "reason" might help soften inevitable clashes.

> Tense situation at home, unless you dissolve easily with a smile, affects relations with everyone else as well; forget hurt feelings; work to increase savings.
> (14 November 1952, Cancer)
> ... be very considerate at home where tension mounts if you display nervousness.
> (19 November 1952, Taurus)
> Use happy feeling early generated to charm loved ones into contentment.
> (19 November 1952, Leo)
> Settle any arguments at home early; then make domicile more attractive for all there; later, discussing family finances, property matters brings better understanding.
> (20 November 1952, Libra)
> Unsatisfactory family, property matter brings you big chance to show your ability to handle personal relations diplomatically, conscientiously. In P.M. plan budget.
> (21 November 1952, Cancer)
> Make sure you are most understanding with members of family who are most distraught.
> (22 November 1952, Scorpio)

Their inevitability, the social reasons of which have been pointed out, is blamed upon the abstract time element, as though at some particular afternoon or evening trouble were brewing at home and the addressee

100

has to exercise particular self-control if he is to avoid a major quarrel. This, of course, reflects also the irrationality of the motives frequently leading to family flare-ups that occur in the wake of entirely insignificant events.

Apart from this appeasement policy, the addressee is encouraged to "take the family out" or to have a "wonderful time" with them by inviting friends; an advice often tendered on holidays when the addressee is likely to do something of the sort anyway. This advice reminds one of the vicarious attempts at institutionalizing pleasure and human closeness, somehow after the fashion of Valentine's Day, Mother's Day and Father's Day. Since it is felt, rightly or wrongly, that the warmth and closeness of the family is on the decline but since the family is retained for both realistic and ideological reasons, the emotional element of warmth and togetherness is rationalistically promoted just as a further means of smoothing out things and keeping the partners together while the actual basis for their common *joie de vivre* seems to have gone. The strange situation in which people have to be pushed in order to do what is supposedly natural – the idea that one has to send flowers to one's wife not because one feels an urge to do so, but because one is afraid of the scene she makes if one forgets the flowers is mirrored by the empty and meaningless nature of the family activities which the columnist sets in motion. He seems to accept thoroughly the idea of "having a wonderful time" by going together to the movies or to a night club.

It might be asked how the column's family policy can be reconciled with our basic assumption that the real addressee is a middle-aged or elderly woman. To this it might be answered that the column, after it has set out to build up the image of a male addressee, has somehow to stick to its guns and to follow up this idea with a fair amount of consistency. No fully satisfactory explanation, however, seems available.

In connection with the family, the role of *neighbors* in the column should be mentioned. They certainly may be expected to be more important in the life of lower-middle-class people than in that of the fictitious successful businessman. It should not be forgotten however, that the column appears in an extremely large city in which social figures, such as the "neighbor" characteristic of primary communities where everyone knows everyone else, are certainly atypical. While the notion of the neighbor may be a simple carry-over from the olden days of the fortune teller who thinks in such terms, it fulfills at the same time the timely function of conjuring up a picture of village-like traditionalism, non-commercial mutual interests and possibly even biblical memories of the neighbor who is like yourself, which all helps to reconcile socially and often psychologically isolated persons with their lot. At the same time, it cannot be ruled out entirely that, as a heritage of the pioneering period in the semi-rural parts of Greater Los Angeles, the neighbor still somehow survives and that there is a positive tradition of neighborly contact and readiness to help each other in the Western United States.

Friends, experts, higher-ups

By far more important than the neighbors, in fact one of the most frequently mentioned topics of the column are the "friends." Their continuous invocation is most conspicuous and calls for tentative explanation even if one assumes that the term "friend" has come to be vastly diluted and is often used as a mere synonym for acquaintance.

More than anything else, the role of the friend in the column may be a carry-over of the crystal-gazer. Astrology's basic assumption of "friendly" and "hostile" conjunctions seems to conjure up human messengers of those powers. But this leaves open why so much is made of the friends while little or nothing is made of the foes. It might be remembered here that one of the most important facets of superstition, direct threat, terrorizing people by some unknown danger and thus inducing them to obey blindly occurs in the material selected very rarely. One has the feeling that the friend–foe dichotomy, which by itself would fit very well into the bi-phasic approach and into a paranoid way of thinking has been subjected to some special censorship and that only the friends have been allowed to survive.

The most important function of the friends in the column may be similar to an image often to be found in fortune telling by cards where someone unexpected turns up and exercises the greatest influence. The friends come from outside, perhaps on account of the columnist's underlying construct that the addressee is unconsciously antagonistic to the family that is generally treated, on an overt level, in stubbornly optimistic terms. They suddenly appear and heap benefits upon the addressee, either by giving him sound advice leading to an increase of his income:

> Vital friend gladly shows you how to enlarge joint venture with limited partner so that better results are produced to mutual advantage; show appreciation by trying suggestions.
> (12 November 1952, Pisces)
> Contact optimistic friends who can aid your advance:
> (22 November 1952, Aries)

or by forthright donations:

> ... a good friend bestows unique benefit.
> (10 November 1952, Virgo)
> Making definite, concrete plan with partners, in public work,
> brings influential friends, support, so success easily obtained.
> (20 November 1952, Cancer)

or by appointments to influential jobs:

> Purposeful friend, eager to see you succeed, brings opportunity for
> you to attain cherished goal.
> (17 November 1952, Capricorn)
> Faithful friends look on you with much favor, seeking to find the
> answer to your present perplexities, which come from expanding
> your consciousness to higher ambitions now.
> (18 November 1952, Aquarius)
> ... later enjoying congenial amusement with serious comrade clears
> path for successful association.
> (19 November 1952, Cancer)
> ... get together with attractive friends who are anxious to aid your
> advance forward.
> (19 November 1952, Pisces)

The general assumption is an extreme expression of dependency needs:
the addressee is invariably advised to follow his friends and is made to
understand that they are stronger than he, know better than he, but will
take care of him.

> Recent, highly active friend believes in you, shows your partner
> how to utilize your talents to greater degree, more constructive
> and effective use.
> (26 November 1952, Gemini)
> Careful, precise friends and potent partners combine to make your
> life more successful. Let them confer favors without interfering
> with their sensible course of action.
> (8 December 1952, Scorpio)
> A generous companion, eager for your advancement, asks good
> friends to study new ways to forward your scientific, educational
> and spiritual aims.
> (3, January 1953, Aquarius)
> Others have the power to make your life a success or failure
> according to the way you handle and impress them with your

financial, practical abilities.

(7 January 1953, Aquarius)

At the same time, potential anxieties and hostilities associated with dependence are removed: the image of those on whom the addressee depends is unequivocally positive. This is the easier the more they are outsiders: the less he knows their shortcomings. The parasitic aspect of dependency is brought out by the continuous reference to benefits to be expected from them. An attempt is made to transform narcissistic losses into the gain of getting rid of the burden of autonomous responsibility and, possibly, adding some masochistic gratifications.

Viewed from this angle, reference to the friends again comes close to the "identification with the aggressor." In fact it may be said that frequently the friends are but rather thin cloaks for the "higher-ups," just as the family is a "screen" for the wife. The rationality of business relations is transfigured into love relationships in which the same ones one has to fear are those who mean one's best and whom therefore one has to love, an obvious transference from the Oedipal situation. Sociologically, it feeds on the awareness that everyone is replaceable in the economic process. The addressee is expected to feel that he is allowed to fulfill his social function as a kind of irrational benefaction given to the undeserving son by an everloving father. The directive given to the underling by his superior is interpreted as though it were given merely in order to help the underling in his failures and weaknesses – an infantile personalization of objectified relationships.

... consult with influential friend about your progress.

(22 November 1952, Cancer)

... influential friend gives good pointer for securing wish, goal.

(1 December 1952, Cancer)

Powerful friend really goes out of way to give you big shove forward, by explaining how he became successful, which can also apply to your choicest hopes. Be attentive.

(8 December 1952, Cancer)

Powerful person unites in confidential arrangement to aid your advance forward toward practical ambitions.

(26 December 1952, Gemini)

Prominent friends, realizing your most out-giving talents, abilities present interesting arrangement for bringing them to attention of all able to bring you success. Cooperate.

(26 December 1952, Cancer)

Much conversation with an official or associate, especially at a

social function or sporting event, reveals your talents so that real
support is quickly given.
   (3 January 1953, Gemini)
Executive, or responsible higher-up, if contacted by you will show
right way to increase and expand present outlets.
   (3 January 1953, Capricorn)
An influential associate, in mood to forward your basic needs,
shows how you can utilize each hour of the day to best advantage.
   (5 January 1953, Cancer)
A prominent person, more practical than you, willingly gives you
good counsel, so listen attentively and follow this improved plan of
action.
   (10 January 1953, Aries)
A powerful man readily gives you a bright new course of action if
you evidence interest. Show your gratitude by following it
carefully.
   (10 January 1953, Taurus)

Here again, the column tends to reinforce guilt feelings, compulsive
patterns and various other unconscious motivations instead of working
against them. It tends to make the socially dependent even more
dependent psychologically. But all this does not exhaust the implications
of the columns idea of the friend. The very vagueness of the term allows
for its psychological utilization in various directions. One of them is the
personalization of society at large. The column is incessantly concerned
with the addressee's compliance with social norms. Their impact can be
mitigated again if they do not appear on an objective but personal level
somewhat reminiscent of the role of the *raisonneur* in the older comedy.
Thus disinterested friends convey to the addressee what has to be done
and what is best for him. They are *like* him, possibly involving the
imagery of himself as well as of siblings on an unconscious level. It seems
quite possible that this function of the friend in the implicit ideology of
the column is related to significant changes in the pattern of authoritarianism which no longer invests real father figures with authority but
replaces them by collectivities. The image of the friend invokes a
collective authority consisting of all those who are like himself, but who
know better since they are not beset by the same worries. There is
something like the idea of the "Big Brother" as the ultimate authority of
totalitarian states, as developed in Orwell's *1984*, involved in the concept
of the friends of the astrological column. Erik H. Erikson has developed
the idea in psychoanalytic terms.[41]

The friends do not enforce anything, but they reveal to the addressee, as it were, that he, in his very isolation, is nevertheless one of them, that he is not isolated at all and that the irrational benefactions they offer him are those offered by the social process itself. This picture of the messenger of society is of course easily fused with that of the higher-up who, in as much as he appeals to duty, is almost invariably a representative of superego demands.

... influential man shows right way to adopt in daily living.
(23 November 1952, Aries)

As to the friends as *projections of the addressee himself*, it stands out that in most cases, they represent his supposedly well-understood self interest in a chemically pure form. It is as though his dialogue with himself when it comes to conflicts would be projected in such a way that he himself is permitted to speak like a child while his "adult" part, his ego, "speaks" to him reassuringly rather than threateningly as a friend in as much as it represents rationality against the momentary urges for pleasure. Yet at the same time, the friends also function in a way for the sake of his id by supposedly fulfilling desires which we may assume he would not dare fulfill himself. It is as though they were telling him, the child: "If you do what we tell you, if you only will be good, we will give you anything you want to have."

Two characteristics of the "friends" may be mentioned in this connection. First, they are often though not always introduced in the plural, which may perhaps be interpreted as sign of their representing either siblings or society at large. Lack of individualization, the notion that everybody can replace everybody else, is also conspicuous. Secondly, the image of the friend is sometimes substituted by that of the stranger or "interesting foreigner," particularly when irrational promises and unexpected gains are concerned. While, on a more overt level, this may reflect the boredom of normal everyday life and resentment of the closed circle of people whom the addressee knows, the figure of the stranger, strongly affect-laden, may play a magical role and may help somehow to overcome suspicion of irrational promises by making their source as irrational as the promises themselves are. Incidentally, only the positive aspect of the stranger is emphasized while the negative one, like all hostility, is entirely repressed by the column. In depth-psychological reasoning one might assume that the kind of person talked to by the column is very in-groupish and does not permit himself any "exogamic" wishes. The mysterious stranger takes care of such repressed urges. It is remarkable, however, that no traces of xenophobia, quite common in astrological magazines, appear in the column. This may best be explained by its "moderation." Only the family background device suggests leanings of this kind. Finally the friend as a stranger may be symbolic of the very fact that an estranged society speaks, as it were, to the addressee.

All these implications lead towards the expectation of some ambivalence toward the friends. It is given vent by the column rather subtly. There is a continuous distinction between "old" and "new" friends and the positive accent is surprisingly enough regularly on the new ones.

> You really want to tell off, force issue with one able to take away your present prestige; instead discuss with unusual associate best way to placate.
>> (10 November 1952, Capricorn)
> Good friend, in distress, looks to you for answer to present obligations; making new acquaintances takes you out of doldrums, brings surprise outlet for your talents.
>> (10 November 1952, Pisces)
> ... make new acquaintances tonight.
>> (18 November 1952, Sagittarius)
> ... make new acquaintances; listen to understand their methods of attaining success.
>> (19 November 1952, Taurus)
> Early get out in the world, make new friends of those different in background.
>> (19 November 1952, Sagittarius)
> ... contact recent acquaintances for best use.
>> (20 November 1952, Taurus)
> Your creative expressions please recent acquaintances who give you opportunity for added avenues, unknown before.
>> (20 November 1952, Virgo)

They to whom one is not yet accustomed, have something of the stranger and foreigner with whom they are sometimes directly identified. At least they are exciting and somehow promise pleasure; in a set-up of standardization and threatening sameness, the idea of the unusual *per se*, is positively cathected. But above all, they fit within the *present*. Conversely, the old friends are at least occasionally presented as a burden, as people who are demanding and who somehow draw unwarranted claims from a relationship that actually belongs to the past.

> Forget working angles with close companions; get out in the world.
>> (13 November 1952, Capricorn)

Old desires, old acquaintances seem for the moment pretty unsatisfactory.
(14 November 1952, Sagittarius)
Ridding life of sinister acquaintance makes more assets obtainable.
(19 November 1952, Scorpio)
Harassed friends try to pull you down to their level; ambitions seem long way off.
(21 November 1952, Sagittarius)

They might be tolerable as "pals" in good days, but the addressee should never take them too seriously, should not allow himself to be involved too deeply with them and is sometimes warned of them outright. Here we might get a glimpse into a strong appeal of the column as well as of the atmosphere of which it is expressive: the rejection of the past. Anything that is no longer "there," that is no longer a fact is treated as absolutely non-existent, in the words of Mephistopheles, "as good as if it had never been there," and to be concerned with the past means only to be distracted from the tasks of the day. In spite of conventional morality and decency, the idea of loyalty is basically rejected by the column: what does not prove useful right here and now is to be abandoned. By applying this method to the "old friends," the hostile phase of the relationship to the friends is rationalized and channelized in a way suitable to the column's over-all pattern of streamlined adjustment. Good are the friends who help you or at least band with you in order to reach some positive goal; the others are really relics of the past, exploit situations which are no longer valid, are therefore moralistically punished and left alone. Such traits reveal something of the cold undercurrent of the slick ideology promoted by the column.[42]

Sometimes the column refers the addressee to the advice of the "expert." The "expert" is a kind of in between the higher-up (or society-at-large) and the closeness of the friend. While he is evaluated on the grounds of his objective merits as the man with the know-how, he is at the same time represented as being above vested interests, solely motivated by his objective knowledge of the matter itself and thus his advice is sugar-coated. The idea of the expert itself has gradually obtained a quasi-magical connotation, of which the column is well aware. Through universal division of labor and extreme specialization he is not solely someone who has gathered special knowledge of some matter but this also involves that it is knowledge which other people, the non-expert, cannot master and in which he nevertheless has to trust implicitly since expertness is supposed to be based exclusively on rational processes.

Thus the expert has gradually grown into the magus of the rationalized world whose authority has to be accepted unquestioningly without violating the taboo set upon blind authority. Since the column has continuously to reckon with the conflict between irrational authoritarian wants and needs and a rationalistic cultural veneer the figure of the expert serves it very well.

> Unnecessary to try to carry all burdens alone; consult with experts, more experienced than self.
> (12 November 1952, Gemini)
> Behind-scenes huddle with personal expert with finances shows way to increase your assets.
> (17 November 1952, Sagittarius)
> Get off with expert who is able to advise best methods to handle tense family problems requiring new approach.
> (20 November 1952, Aquarius)
> ... be economical in expenditures, cooperative with tax-experts.
> (22 November 1952, Libra)

The key figures in all personal relations as viewed by the column are the *higher-ups*, the bosses, both in their capacity in business life and in their psychological role of father substitutes; it is a safe guess that a very high percentage of all references to humans contained in the column, even if veiled by some of the categories so far discussed, actually refers to the higher-ups. Thus, during a sample period from 10 November to 22 November the categories of human beings mentioned by the column can be broken down as follows:

Category	Number of times mentioned	
Strangers		1
Neighbor		2
Expert		5
Family		35
Friend	overlapping {	53
Higher-up		48

Of course, they are treated more ambivalently and bi-phasically than the "friends." On the one hand, they are a continuous threat mainly because they want some "accounting;" one has obligations towards them often beyond one's capacity, and has to obey them. But they are also blamed on a personal level for being pompous, pretentious and what not. Both threats, however, are mitigated, the objective one by reference either to the moral right or to the better insight of the higher-ups, their whims and irrationalities by the implication that they too have their worries, their inner problems which call for understanding or that they are simply ridiculous in as much as they are pompous or inflated personalities. Thus conflicts appear as though they need not be taken too seriously:

... harassed higher-up who needs your perseverance to complete tough assignment.
(14 November 1952, Capricorn)
Annoyance over drudgeries eased by aiding worried associate with harder problems.
(16 November 1952, Gemini)

Often the friend's power is invoked as mitigating intermediary, softening up the higher-ups or taking the strain out of the relation:

... painstaking friend cooperates with associates to bring your wish.
(11 November 1952, Scorpio)
... good friend willingly gives pointers best way you can secure personal ambitions.
(17 November 1952, Aquarius)

The attitude toward the higher-ups recommended to the addressee is practically without exception that of giving in and respecting the hierarchical order. One of the favorite suggestions is to placate the higher-ups, the way a child would act towards his parents when they are "cross." The emphasis is less on the fulfillment of duties *per se* as it is on a shrewd and flexible psychological attitude. The higher-ups must be "treated" skillfully, if one wants to keep in their good graces. In a genuinely hierarchical fashion, the relationship is depicted as that of the court favorite who wants to ingratiate himself with the princeling rather than to do his work satisfactorily.

... keep steadfast in impressing higher-up with your innate abilities.
(10 November 1952, Aquarius)
... increase prestige by aiding officials, executives to make their jobs

110

more successful.

(13 November 1952, Aquarius)

At times the ungrumbling attitude towards superiors takes the paradoxical aspect of bribery. The weaker is supposed to invite the stronger,
to take him out and to indulge in similar ventures in order to, as it is put
euphemistically, achieve a satisfactory human relationship.[43]

> ... invite powerful persons into your home.
> (13 December 1952, Leo)
> ... bring into open your appreciation of higher-ups.
> (24 December 1952, Taurus)
> Attend a distinguished party or gathering; entertain influential
> individuals if time permits.
> (13 January 1953, Capricorn)
> Invite influential higher-ups to party and impress with your
> abilities.
> (18 January 1953, Libra)

It is as though the notion of neo-feudalism which lurks in the back of the
columnist's mind, would carry with itself the association of the serfs
paying tribute to the master – an idea equally retrogressive socially and
psychologically. Of course, the rationalization is always the egalitarian
one that the higher-up and the addressee are socially on an equal footing
and that the latter can invite his boss without any hesitation. The hint that
such service will be appreciated is rarely absent.

This idea is in accordance with the other pole of the bi-phasic
approach to the higher-up. If the friends are often mere cloaks of the
superiors, the higher-ups are frequently presented as friends somewhat
reminiscent of a stern and demanding father who would use the intervals
of his tyranny in order to assure his kids that he is their best friend and
oppresses them only for their own sake. This goes together with a
glorification of the image of the higher-up whose position of success is
supposed to be the result of his innate qualities, as though those who have
the office had also the brain (*Wem Gott ein Amt gibt, dem gibt er auch den
Verstand*: on whom God bestows an office, he also bestows intelligence).
Thus hierarchical relationships are mirrored by the column in an apologetic and fetishistic manner.

> Friends, partners, opponents will listen with reason to any
> intelligent plan you submit, for they are open-minded, willing to
> replace hardheaded attitude with joint arrangement.
> (2 December 1952, Aries)

111

Executive, official very exact about every detail irks your lofty aims but shows right way for you to attain worldly honor, popularity, credit.

(3 December 1952, Leo)

Meticulous executive, high-up shows how routines can be expanded wisely.

(8 December 1952, Sagittarius)

A "dressing down" by executive, official or government is fine for it shows you how you are now faring financially.

(10 January 1953, Aquarius)

Often simple prestige terms such as "important personality" are employed in order to add a halo to the higher-ups' more favorable position.

... influential executive.	(10 November 1952, Scorpio)
... influential executive.	(26 November 1952, Aries)
... prominent persons.	(22 December 1952, Libra)
... prominent person.	(24 December 1952, Capricorn)
... driving, important person.	(22 January 1952, Gemini)

The more generalized attitude to be derived from the dependent, shrewdly meek attitude towards the higher-ups is one of general reconciliation, particularly of placating opponents, of "playing up" to them. The columnist figures that to a degree everybody fails to live up to his duties and lays himself open to some kind of scolding either by an insatiable superior or by a nagging wife. Whenever the reader runs into such difficulties, he should, according to the column, not allow things to come to a head, but rather to seek a way out of it by taking a conciliatory attitude, talking in a friendly manner and winning over opponents who might finally be his best friends. The idea of *talking* plays an important role in this respect. This is a final corroboration of the weight of orality within the psychological concept of the column. The addressee is encouraged to speak, speaking itself being a hybrid between a passive giving-in attitude and the aggressive impulses to "speak up against somebody." This advice is the more promising since the oppressed really want to speak in the depth of their heart but have to repress this wish. An attempt is being made to put this urge into the service of realism and conformity.

The net result of the practice furthered by the column is that conflicts should either be altogether avoided or settled by clever meekness – in fact, by a behavior reminiscent of that of the woman who wants to get the better of the man on whom she depends. By contrast, there are no concrete references to autonomous and independent behavior.

CONCLUSION

In view of the limited and highly specific nature of the material scrutinized, no "generalization" in the strict sense seems to be possible. However, the material suggests certain perspectives of a somewhat broader nature. While largely having been drawn as inferences from the specific interpretations attempted, they should also provide a background for the whole study and particularly make it understandable why it was carried through.

Though we are not primarily interested in astrology *per se*, as was pointed out before, it may be well to remember that the astrological fad, and analogous ones, is widespread enough and exercises sufficient influence as to warrant an investigation of its own. Though an increase of the astrological fashion cannot be "proved" for obvious reasons, since no comparative figures from the past are available, it seems quite likely. Thus, in German newspapers, the signs of the zodiac under which a person was born have come to be frequently mentioned in lonely-hearts advertisements. If one attributes such an increase to the mounting exploitation of superstitious leanings alone, a higher distribution of astrological material, this seems hardly to suffice as an explanation since this increase of material would scarcely work unless there were some definite susceptibility for it among the people. It is this susceptibility much more than astrology as such which deserves attention; we want to utilize our studies of astrology as a kind of key to more widespread social and psychological potentialities. In other words, we want to analyze astrology in order to find out what it indicates as a "symptom" of some tendencies of our society as well as of typical psychological trends among those this society embraces.

Obviously, the first concept that comes to mind in this connection is that of social and psychological dependence. Our analysis of the *Los Angeles Times* column has pointed out in detail how dependency needs of the audience are presupposed, fostered and exploited continuously. However, in terms of the specificity of contemporary astrology, the concept of dependence as such seems to be somewhat too abstract as to lead us very far. Throughout history in organized society, the majority of people were somehow dependent and in some phases probably more so than today. This, however, has to be somewhat qualified. No matter whether the individual is "freer" today in many respects than he used formerly to be, the socialization of life, the "seizure" of the individual by innumerable channels of organization has certainly increased. Suffice it to state as an illustration that the traditional dichotomy between work and

113

leisure tends to become more and more reduced and that socially controlled "leisure activities" take over more and more of the individual's spare time. While the basic dependence of the individual on the social body, and in a highly irrational form, has always prevailed, this dependence was at least "veiled" to many people during the classical era of liberalism where people had come to think of themselves as self-sustaining monads. This veil has now been drawn apart and people begin to face their own dependence much more than they used to 80 years ago; largely because the processes of social control are no longer those of an anonymous market which decides the economic fate of the individual in terms of offer and demand. The intermediary processes between social control and the individual tend to vanish and the individual has once again to obey the direct verdict of the groups at the helm of society. It may be this mounting obviousness of dependence rather than an increase of dependence *per se* which makes itself felt today and prepares the minds of the people for astrology as well as for totalitarian creeds. Paradoxically, a higher amount of insight might result in a reversion to attitudes that prevailed long before the rise of modern capitalism. For, while people recognize their dependence and often enough venture the opinion that they are mere pawns, it is extremely difficult for them to face this dependence unmitigated. Society is made of those whom it comprises. If the latter would fully admit their dependence on man-made conditions, they would somehow have to blame themselves, would have to recognize not only their impotence but also that they are the cause of this impotence and would have to take responsibilities which today are extremely hard to take. This may be one of the reasons why they like so much to project their dependence upon something else, be it a conspiracy of Wall Street bankers or the constellation of the stars. What drives people into the arms of the various kinds of "prophets of deceit" is not only their sense of dependence and their wish to attribute this dependence to some "higher" and ultimately more justifiable sources, but it is also their wish to reinforce their own dependence, not to have to take matters into their own hands – a wish, true, which is ultimately engendered by the pressure under which they live. One may say that the adepts of astrology frequently play and overplay their dependence; a hypothesis which would fit well with the observation that so many followers of astrology do not seem quite to believe but rather take an indulgent, semi-ironical attitude towards their own conviction. In other words, astrology cannot be simply interpreted as an expression of dependence but must be also considered as an *ideology for dependence*, as an attempt to strengthen and somehow justify painful conditions which seem to be more tolerable if an affirmative attitude is taken towards them. Anyhow, the world appears to most people today more as a "system" than ever before, covered by an all-comprising net of organization with no loopholes where the individual could "hide" in face of the ever-present demands and tests of a society ruled by a hierarchical business set-up and coming pretty close to what we called "*verwaltete Welt*," a world caught by administration.

It is this reality situation which has so many and obvious similarities with paranoid systems of thinking that it seems to invite such patterns of intellectual behavior, as well as compulsive attitudes. The similarity between the social and the paranoid system consists not only of the closedness and centralized structure as such but also of the fact that the "system" under which most people feel they work has to them an irrational aspect itself. That is to say, they feel that everything is linked up with everything else and that they have no way out, but at the same time the whole mechanism is so complicated that they fail to understand its *raison d'être* and even more, they suspect that this closed and systematic organization of society does not really serve their wants and needs, but has a fetishistic, self-perpetuating "irrational" quality, strangely alienated from the life that is thus being structured. Thus people even of supposedly "normal" mind are prepared to accept systems of delusions for the simple reason that it is too difficult to distinguish such systems from the equally inexorable and equally opaque one under which they actually have to live out their lives. This is pretty well reflected by astrology as well as by the two brands of totalitarian states which also claim to have a key for everything, know all the answers, reduce the complex to simple and mechanical inferences, doing away with anything that is strange and unknown and at the same time fail to explain anything.

The system thus characterized, the "*verwaltete Welt*," has a threatening aspect *per se*. In order to do full justice to such needs as the one satisfied by astrology, one has to be aware of the ever-threatening impact of society. The feeling of being "caught," the impossibility for most people to regard themselves by any stretch of imagination as the masters of their own fate, is only one of the elements of this threat. Another one, more deep-lying both psychologically and sociologically, is that our social system, in spite of its closedness and the ingenuity of its technological functioning, seems actually to move towards self-destruction. The sense of an underlying crisis has never disappeared since the First World War and most people realize, at least dimly, that the continuity of the social process and somehow of their own capacity of reproducing their life, is no longer due to supposedly "normal" economic processes but to factors

115

such as universal rearmament, which by themselves breed destruction while they are apparently the only means of self-perpetuation. This sense of threat is real enough and some of its expressions such as the A and H bombs are about to outrun the wildest neurotic fears and destructive fantasies. The more people profess official optimism, the more profoundly they are probably affected by this mood of doom, the idea, correct or erroneous, that the present state of affairs somehow must lead towards a total explosion and that the individual can do very little about it. The sense of doom may today obtain a peculiarly sinister coloring by the fact that the present form of social existence seems to go down whereas no new and higher form of social organization appears on the horizon. The "wave of the future" seems to consummate the very fears that are produced by the conditions of the present. Astrology takes care of this mood by translating it into a pseudo-rational form, thus somehow localizing free-floating anxieties in some definite symbolism, but it also gives some vague and diffused comfort by making the senseless appear as though it had some hidden and grandiose sense while at the same time corroborating that this sense can neither be sought in the realm of the human nor can properly be grasped by humans. The combination of the realistic and the irrational in astrology may ultimately be accounted for by the fact it represents a threat and a remedy in one, just as certain psychotics may start a fire and at the same time prepare for its extinction.

In spite of this comfort, astrology mirrors exactly the opaqueness of the empirical world and implies so little transcendent faith, is so opaque itself that it can be easily accepted by supposedly sceptical, disillusioned people. The intellectual attitude it is expressive of is one of disoriented agnosticism. The cult of God has been replaced by the cult of facts, just as the fatal entities of astrology, the stars, are themselves viewed as facts, things, ruled by mechanical laws. One could not grasp the specificity of astrology and of the whole frame of mind it stands for if one would simply call it a reversion to older states of metaphysics: what it is characteristic of is the transfiguration of a world of things into quasi-metaphysical powers. Auguste Comte's postulate that positivism should become a kind of religion is fulfilled ironically – science is hypostatized as an ultimate, absolute truth. The astrologist, as was pointed out in our brief survey of magazines, is very anxious to present it as a science. It may be mentioned in passing that just as adherents of philosophical empiricism seem to be more susceptible for organized secondary superstition than speculative thinkers, extreme empiricism, teaching absolute obedience of the mind to given data, "facts," has no principle such as the idea of reason, by which to distinguish the possible from the impossible, and thus the development of enlightenment overreaches itself and produces a mentality often no longer able to resist mythological temptations. It may also be mentioned that the modern science, which has replaced more and more categories which once interpreted events as though they were meaningful, tends to promote a kind of opaqueness which at least for the uninitiated is hard to distinguish from an equally opaque and non-transparent thesis such as the dependence of the individual human fate on stellar constellations. While the astrological way of thinking is indicative of a "disillusioned" world, it enhances disillusion by surrendering the idea of the human even more completely to blind nature than it actually is.

Yet astrology is not merely an enlarged duplicate of an opaque and reified world. While people have come to be conditioned in such a way as to be unable to think or conceive of anything that is not like the existent, they want at the same time desperately to get away from the existent. The drabness of a commodity society which does not allow any quality to exist for its own sake, but levels down everything to a function of universal exchange seems to be unbearable and any panacea is embraced that promises to gild it. Instead of the complicated, strenuous and difficult intellectual processes which might overcome the feeling of drabness by understanding what really makes the world so drab, a desperate short-cut is sought which offers both spurious understanding and flight into a supposedly higher realm. More than in any other respect, astrology resembles in this dimension other mass media such as the movies: its message appears as something metaphysically meaningful, something where the spontaneity of life is being restored while actually reflecting the very same reified conditions which seem to be dispensed with through an appeal to the "absolute." The comparison of astrology with religious mysticism, dubious in more than one respect, is invalid particularly in as much as the mystery celebrated by astrology is empty – the movements of the stars, supposedly explaining everything, explain nothing and even if the whole hypothesis were true it would have to be explained why and how the stars come to determine human life, an explanation that hasn't even been attempted by astrology. A veneer of scientific rationality has been fused with blind acceptance of un-demonstrable contentions and the spurious exaltation of the factual.

This strange structure of astrology is significant, however, because it can itself be reduced to an all-important mundane structure: the division of labor which is basic to the whole life process of society. One may well concede that the isolated elements of astrology are rational. On the one hand, there are stars and their laws as explored by the science of astronomy, and the astrologists seem to take care to keep their statements, as far as they are concerned with celestial events, strictly in line with those movements which actually take place according to astronomy. On the other hand, there is the empirical life of man, particularly with regard to typical social situations and psychological conflicts, and our analysis has shown that the astrologists display quite a keen and sensible insight into life; that they speak out of experience, without any traces of delusion. The "mystery" of astrology, in other words, the element of irrationality and, incidentally, the sole element that accounts for its mass appeal, is the way these two "unrelated" realms are related to each other. There is nothing irrational about astrology except its decisive contention that these two spheres of rational knowledge are interconnected, whereas not the slightest evidence of such an interconnection can be offered. This mystery, however, is not merely "superstition." It is the negative expression of the organization of work, and, more specifically of the organization of science. There is but one world and its division into disconnected spheres is not due to being as such, but to the organization of human knowledge of being. It is in a way "arbitrary," though unavoidable in terms of historical development, to keep, say, the science of astronomy and the science of psychology completely apart. This arbitrariness leaves its scars in knowledge itself; there is a break between the two sciences, continuity ends for all practical purposes and the systematic attempts at a unification of the sciences remain extraneous and formalistic. The awareness of the gap is reflected by astrology. On the one hand, it is an attempt, once again in short-cut fashion, to bridge the gap and to relate, with a stroke, what is unrelated and what, one ultimately feels, must somehow be linked together. On the other hand, the very fact that the two realms *are* unrelated, that there is a void between them, a kind of no-man's-land, affords an ideal opportunity to settle there and to come forward with unsubstantiated claims. It is in fact this very unrelatedness, the irrationality in the relations between astronomy and psychology, for which there is no common denominator, no "rationale," which affords astrology with the semblance of justification in its pretense to be mysterious, irrational knowledge itself. The opaqueness of astrology is nothing but the opaqueness prevailing between various scientific areas which could not be meaningfully brought together. Thus one might say that irrationality is in itself the outgrowth of the principle of rationalization which was evolved for the sake of higher efficiency, the division of labor. What Spengler called the modern caveman, dwells in the cavity, as it were, between organized sciences which do not cover the universality of existence.[44]

118

Of course, the basic deception, the arbitrary connection of the disconnected, could easily be grasped in terms of present scientific knowledge. But it is significant of the situation that this knowledge is actually "esoteric" in as much as few people seem to be capable of drawing such consequences, whereas self-styled esoteric knowledge such as astrology has come to be extremely popular. It was pointed out before that astrology, just like racism and other intellectual sects, presupposes a state of semi-erudition. When evaluating astrology as a symptom of the decline of erudition, however, one has to be cautious not to indulge in superficial statements of official cultural pessimism. It would be irresponsible to allege such a decline in general and quantitative terms, not only because no valid comparison with former periods seems to be possible, but also because in many respects erudition is likely to be more widespread today than it used to be, i.e., layers of the population which formerly had no access to culture and knowledge are now brought into contact with the arts and sciences through the modern means of mass communications. The state of mind that can properly be called semi-erudite seems to be indicative of a structural change rather than of the distribution of cultural facilities. What is really happening is that, concomitantly with the ever-increasing belief in "facts," information has a tendency to replace intellectual penetration and reflection. The element of "synthesis" in the classical philosophical sense seems to be more and more lacking; there is, on the one hand, a wealth of material and knowledge, but the relationship is more one of formal order and classification than one which would open up the supposedly stubborn facts by interpretation and understanding. The rigid dichotomy maintained in very influential philosophical schools today between logical formalism and a kind of empiricism that regards every theory only as the expression of expectations to be fulfilled by data later to be found is symptomatic of this intellectual situation. It is, in a way, mirrored by astrology too, and it may well be said that astrology presents the bill for the neglect of interpretative thinking for the sake of fact gathering. There are, on the one hand, the "facts" both of stellar movements and well-known psychological reactions, but there is no real synthesis even attempted, no relationship that makes sense is established – and probably cannot be established between two spheres so widely divergent. Instead an entirely extraneous subsumption of human events under astronomical laws is attempted, externalization, as will be remembered, being an essential facet of astrology in all respects. The element of semi-erudition shows itself in the failure of the mind to recognize the fallacy not of the material thus interconnected, but of the spuriousness of the link. Lack of "understanding," disorientation in a complex and at the same time fatal social set-up and also, possibly, confusion created through misunderstandings of the recent developments of natural sciences (particularly of the replacement of the concept of matter by that of energy which seems to invite wild constructs) contribute to the readiness to relate the unrelated – a pattern of thinking which, by the way, is well-known to psychiatry. Under this viewpoint, astrology may well be defined as an organized system of "ideas of reference." While the naive persons who take more or less for granted what happens hardly ask the questions astrology pretends to answer and while really educated and intellectually fully developed persons would look through the fallacy of astrology, it is an ideal stimulus for those who have started to reflect, who are dissatisfied with the veneer of mere existence and who are looking for a "key," but who are at the same time incapable of the sustained intellectual effort required by theoretical insight and also lack the critical training without which it would be utterly futile to attempt to understand what is happening. Precisely this type, both sceptical and insufficiently equipped intellectually, a type hardly capable of integrating the various intellectual functions torn apart by the division of labor seems to be on the upsurge today. Thus astrology is an expression of the impasse reached by the division of intellectual labor not only in objective terms, according to its intrinsic structure, but also subjectively, being directed at those whose minds have been conditioned and warped by that division of labor. The astrological fad can mainly be explained as the commercial exploitation of this frame of mind, both presupposing and corroborating retrogressive tendencies. In as far as it is part and parcel of the all-comprising pattern of cultural industry; in fact, the specific ideology promoted by a publication such as the *Los Angeles Times* column is pretty much the same as that emerging from the movies and television although the type of people at which it aims is probably somewhat different – there is some "division of labor" also among the various mass media, mainly with regard to the various kinds of customers which each medium attempts to ensnare. Primarily, astrological publications "sell" due to the objective and subjective characteristics so far outlined. In view of this commercial success, astrology is taken up by more powerful economic agencies which take it away from the crystal-gazer atmosphere, as it were (just as the big studios took away the movies from the amusement park booths), purge it of its manifestly crazy traits, make it "respectable" and thus utilize it commercially on a large scale. This, of course, is only possible in as much as the inherent ideology of astrology harmonizes with what the interests vested in this area want to promote. It is of little importance whether, as it seems likely, conformity and obedience is *a priori* inherent in astrology or whether the ideology spotted by our analysis of the *Los Angeles Times* column is due to astrology's integration into a larger ideological framework.

Speaking in general terms, the astrological ideology resembles, in all its major characteristics, the mentality of the "high scorers" of the "Authoritarian Personality." It was, in fact, this similarity which induced us to undertake the present study. Apart from the features brought out in our analysis, some more traits of the high scorer cropping up in the column may be mentioned. Here goes the over-all externalization promoted by astrology, the idea that everything negative is due only to external, mostly physical circumstances, but that otherwise "everything is fine," the continuous stress on conventional wholesomeness. All this is indicative of rigid psychological defenses against instinctual urges. The psychological syndrome, however, expressed by astrology and propagandized by its advice is only the means to an end, the promotion of a social ideology. It offers the advantage of veiling all deeper-lying causes of distress and thus promoting acceptance of the given. Moreover, by strengthening the sense of fatality, dependence and obedience, it paralyzes the will to change objective conditions in any respect and relegates all worries to a private plane promising a cure-all by the very same compliance which prevents a change of conditions. It can easily be seen how well this suits the over-all purpose of the prevailing ideology of today's cultural industry; to reproduce the *status quo* within the mind of the people.

It should not be overlooked that within the total set-up of the ideology of mass culture astrology represents a "specialty." The nucleus of its doctrine as well as of its adherents shows many characteristics of a sect. But just this sect-like character, the claim of something particular and apocryphal to be all-comprehensive and exclusive, is indicative of a most sinister social potential: the transition of an emasculated liberal ideology to a totalitarian one. Just as those who can read the phony signs of the stars believe that they are in the know, the followers of totalitarian parties believe that their special panaceas are universally valid and feel justified in imposing them as a general rule. The paradoxical idea of a one-party state – while the idea of "party," being derived from "part" is itself indicative of a plurality – is the consummation of a trend feebly presaged by the opinionated, inaccessible attitude of the astrological adept who defends his creed by hook or crook without ever entering into a real argument, who has auxiliary hypotheses in order to defend himself even where his statements are blatantly erroneous and who ultimately cannot be spoken to, can probably not be reached at all and lives on a kind of narcissistic island.

It is this aspect which ultimately justifies the psychiatric emphasis given to our study, the interest psychiatry has to take in astrology and the psychiatric nature of many of our interpretations. Again, great care has to be taken not to oversimplify the relationship between astrology and psychosis. Some of the complexities of this relationship have been stated in the text itself. It should be emphasized that there is neither justification for primitively calling adepts of astrology psychotics, while, as has been shown, it also serves the function of a defense against psychosis, nor to postulate that astrology as such is indicative of people becoming crazier and crazier, or that paranoia as such is on the increase. However, the hypothesis may be ventured that various historical situations and social settings favor various psychological syndromes and "bring out" and accentuate distinct types of possibilities ever-present in human beings. Thus nineteenth-century liberalism with the idea of the small independent entrepreneur who accumulates wealth by saving has probably elicited character formations of the anal type more than, say, the eighteenth century, where the ego ideal was more largely determined by the feudal characterological imagery which would be called in Freudian terms "genital"[45] – although closer scrutiny would probably show that this aristocratic ego ideal hardly had so much basis in fact as romantic desires would have it be the case. Anyway, it seems that in eras of decline of social systems, with the insecurity and anxiety widespread in such eras, paranoid tendencies in people are evinced and often channelized by institutions wishing to distract such tendencies from their objective reasons. Thus organized flagellantism and apocalyptic fantasies among the masses were characteristic of the first phase of the decay of the feudal system, and witch-hunting of the period of Counter Reformation when an attempt was being made to artificially reconstruct a social order that by that time had become obsolete. Similarly, today's world, which offers such a strong reality basis for everybody's sense of being persecuted, calls for paranoic characters. Hitler was certainly psychologically abnormal, but it was just this abnormality which created the spell that allowed his success with the German masses. It may well be said that it is precisely the element of madness that paralyzes and attracts followers of mass movements of all kinds; a structure to which it is a corollary that people never quite fully believe what they pretend to believe and therefore overdo their own beliefs, prone to translate them into violent action at short notice. The movement "moral rearmament" would never have gained its momentum by its general humanitarian aims alone, but its exhibitionist rite of public confession and its hostile attitude against sex, so strongly reminiscent of the strengthening of defenses throughout other mass media, seems to act as a real stimulus. One may well compare the function of these confessions to the forced confessions of the supposed traitors in Russia and the satellite states behind the iron curtain, which far from disillusioning Communist followers in the free world often seem to cast a kind of magic spell and to be swallowed hook, line and sinker. Astrology has to be regarded as a little model of much greater social feeding on paranoid dispositions. Thus far it is a symptom of retrogression of society as a whole which allows some insight into the illness itself. It denotes a recurrence of the unconscious, steered for purposes of social control which is finally irrational itself.

Perhaps it may be regarded as symbolic that, at the beginning of the era that seems to come to its end, the philosopher Leibniz who was the first to introduce the concept of the unconscious, was also the one who stated that, notwithstanding his tolerant and peaceable mind – he sometimes signed himself Pacidius – he felt profound contempt only for those activities of the mind which aimed at deception and named as the main example for such activities astrology.

NOTES

The editor's notes, or editorial additions to Adorno's notes, are enclosed in square brackets.

1   [R.M. Brickner, *Is Germany Incurable?* New York: J.B. Lippincott, 1943.]
2   Sigmund Freud, *Collected Papers*, trans. by Joan Riviere (London, 1949), IV, pp. 368–407. [All Adorno's citations of Freud have been referenced to the appropriate volume of *The Standard Edition of the Complete Psychological Works of Sigmund Freud*, (ed. J Strachey). London: Hogarth Press, 1953–74. In this case: *SE* 17.]
3   [G. Devereux (ed.), *Psychoanalysis and the Occult*. New York: International Universities Press, 1953. Reprinted London: Souvenir Press, 1974.]
4   Charles H. Cooley, *Social Organization* (New York, 1909) [reprinted with an intro. by P. Rieff, New York: Schocken Books, 1962], chapter III. Cf. also Robert E. Park and Ernest W. Burgess, *Introduction to the Science of Sociology* (Chicago [:University of Chicago Press], 1921), pp. 50, 56–7, 282–7.
5   [*SE* 18.]
6   It should be noted that the oafish attitude taken by the magazines against what it regards inferior remnants of outdated superstition does not prevent it from at least a kind of official solidarity with competing rackets of a pseudoscientific tinge of our own time. Good fellowship among all those occupied with esoteric knowledge is promoted. One serious reference is made to "our numerological friends."
7   The uniformity of the material, though it has certainly its psychological

aspects or those of psychological calculation, is probably explained primarily by the fact that the magazines are published by a very few centralized agencies.

8 [See E. Simmel, 'Anti-Semitism and Mass Psychopathology,' in E. Simmel (ed.), *Anti-Semitism: A Social Disease*. New York: International Universities Press, 1946.]

9 In some respects he is in a position similar to that of the political demagogue who has to make some promises to everybody and has to figure out what is likely to worry most the majority of his audience.

10 By pseudo-individualization we mean endowing cultural mass production with a halo of free choice or open market on the basis of standardization itself. T.W. Adorno, "On Popular Music," *Studies in Philosophy and Social Science*. IX, 1941, p. 25.

11 Theodor Reik, *Listening with the Third Ear* (New York [: Garden City Books], 1949), pp. 458–63. Reik applies the term to the jargon of semi-professionals. This jargon has, in the meantime, become socialized.

12 *Studies in Philosophy and Social Science* [IX.1] 1941. [See also H. Herzog, 'What do we really know about daytime serial listeners?', P.F. Lazarsfeld and F.N. Stanton (eds), *Radio Research 1942–1943*. New York: Duell, Sloane & Peace, 1944.]

13 Observations of a closely related nature were presented in the paper "Psychiatric Theory and Institutional Context," read by Dr. Alfred H. Stanton at the 109th Annual meeting of the American Psychiatric Association, Los Angeles, 7 May 1953.

14 Sigmund Freud, *Werke*, XIV (London, 1948), "Einige psychische Folgen des anatomischen Geschlechtsunterschieds," pp. 24f. ['Some Psychological Consequences of the Anatomical Distinction Between the Sexes', *SE* 19]; *Werke*, X (London, 1940), "Neue Folge der Vorlesungen zur Einführung in die Psychoanalyse," pp. 134f. ['New Introductory Lectures on Psychoanalysis,' Lecture 23, 'Femininity,' *SE* 22.]

15 Sigmund Freud, *Werke*, VII (London, 1941), "Zwangshandlungen und Religionsübungen," pp. 129ff. ['Obsessive Actions and Religious Practices,' *SE* 9]; *Werke*, IV, "Ueber libidinose Typen," p. 511 ['Libidinal Types,' *SE* 21.]

16 Erich Fromm, "Zum Gefühl der Ohnmacht," *Zeitschrift für Sozialforschung*, VI, 1937, and T. W. Adorno, "On Popular Music," *op. cit.*

17 Cf. Sigmund Freud, *Werke*, XV (London, 1940), "Angst und Triebleben," pp. 105f. ['New Introductory Lectures on Psychoanalysis,' Lecture 32, 'Anxiety and Instinctual Life,' *SE* 22.]

18 Cf. Sigmund Freud, *Werke*, XV, "Neue Folge der Vorlesungen zur Einfuhrung in die Psychoanalyse," p. 108 ['New Introductory Lectures on Psychoanalysis', Lecture 32, 'Anxiety and Instinctual Life', *SE* 22]; *Werke*, VII, "Charakter und Analerotik," pp. 203f. ['Character and Anal Eroticism', *SE* 19.]

19 Cf. Sigmund Freud, *Werke*, XII (London, 1940), "Vorlesungen zur Einführung in die Psychoanalyse," pp. 369f. ['Introductory Lectures on Psychoanalysis,' Lecture 22, 'Development and Regression,' *SE* 16]; *Werke*, XIII (London, 1940), "Jenseits des Lustprinzips," pp. 3ff. ['Beyond the Pleasure Principle,' *SE* 18.]

20 Erich Fromm, "Zum Gefühl der Ohnmacht," *Zeitschrift für Sozialforschung*, VI, 1937, pp. 103–4.
21 Otto Fenichel, *Psychoanalytic Theory of Neuroses* (New York, 1945) [London: Routledge & Kegan Paul, 1946], p. 153f.
22 Ibid., p. 270.
23 Ibid., p. 291.
24 Wolfenstein and Leites, *Movies* (Glencoe, 1950), p. 21. [M. Wolfenstein and N. Leites, *Movies: A Psychoanalytic Study*. Glencoe: Free Press, 1950.]
25 Cf. Herrmann Nunberg, "Ichstarke und Ichschwache," *Internationale Zeitschrift für Psychoanalyse*, XXIV, 1939.
26 [H. Bergson, *Le Rire: essai sur la signification du comique*. Paris: Alcan, 1924.]
27 This dichotomy goes back to the characterological typology developed by C.G. Jung (*Psychologische Typen*. Zurich, 1921, pp. 473ff.) ['Psychological Types' in his *Complete Works* 6. London: Routledge & Kegan Paul, 1971]. It should be emphasized that just such a psychologist who claimed to give metaphysical depth to supposedly shallow psychoanalytic concepts, is particularly prone to be taken up by commercial popularization.
28 Cf. Sigmund Freud, *Werke*, XI (London, 1940), "Vorlesungen zur Einführung in die Psychoanalyse," pp. 426ff. ['Introductory Lectures on Psychoanalysis,' Lecture 26, 'The Libido Theory and Narcissism,' *SE* 16.]
29 Cf. Karen Horney, *New Ways in Psychoanalysis* (New York [:Norton], 1940); *Neurosis and Human Growth* (New York, 1950) [London: Routledge & Kegan Paul, 1951].
30 It may be mentioned in passing that the historical origins of the concept of intuition coincide with the extreme great rationalistic systems of seventeenth century philosophy. Thus to Spinoza, intuition is the highest type of knowledge, though the term is used by him in a sense somewhat different from the current one. In Leibniz, the concept of the unconscious is introduced by way of mathematical reflections on subliminal knowledge under the title of "petites perceptions." The history of intuitionism is the night side of accidental rationalism.
31 [A French 'adventurer' in Lessing's comedy *Minna von Barnhelm*. See G.E. Lessing, *Gesammelte Werke*, Band 2. Berlin: Aufbau, 1968.]
32 [K. Mannheim, *Man and Society*. Routledge & Kegan Paul, 1940 (reprinted 1980).]
33 Cf. T.W. Adorno, Else Frenkel-Brunswik, Daniel Levinson, Nevitt R. Sanford [*The Authoritarian Personality*] (New York: [Harper & Row], 1950).
34 A study on science fiction would be worthwhile. This widespread fad may owe its tremendous popularity to its ingenious solution of the conflict between irrationality and common sense. The science fiction reader need no longer feel ashamed of being a superstitious and gullible person. The fantasies of his own making, no matter how irrational they are, and how much projective content of either individual or collective nature may be implied, appear no longer as irreconcilable to reality. Thus, the term "another world" which once had a metaphysical meaning, is here brought down to the level of astronomy and obtains an empirical ring. Ghosts and horrible threats often reviving repulsive freakish entities of olden times, are treated as natural and scientific objects coming out of space from another star and preferably from another galaxy although to the best of today's biological knowledge, the "law

of convergence" would probably lead even on distant stars to developments much more similar to those on earth than it appears in the secularizations of demonology enjoyed by the science fiction reader. Man's own reification and mechanization is projected back upon reality in the very widespread robot literature. Incidently, science fiction consummates a long tradition of Amencan literature dealing with the irrational while at the same time denying its irrationality. Edgar Allan Poe is in various respects the inventor of science fiction, no less than of the detective story.

35 Cf. Sigmund Freud, *Werke*, XI, "Vorlesungen zur Einführung in die Psychoanalyse," pp. 211ff.; 341ff. ['Introductory Lectures on Psychoanalysis, Lecture 13, 'Archaic and Infantile Features in Dreams,' *SE* 15; Lecture 21, 'Development of the Libido and Sexual Organisations,' *SE* 16.]

36 Cf. Sigmund Freud, *Werke*, XI, "Vorlesungen zur Einführung in die Psychoanalyse," pp. 383f. ['Introductory Lectures on Psychoanalysis,' Lecture 22, 'Paths to the Formation of Symptoms,' *SE* 16]; *Werke*, XIV, "Hemmung, Symptom und Angst," pp. 136f. ['The Problem of Anxiety,' *SE* 20]; *Werke*, XV, "Neue Folgen der Vorlesungen zur Einführung in die Psychoanalyse," pp. 93f. ['New Introductory Lectures on Psychoanalysis,' Lecture 32, 'Anxiety and Instinctual Life,' *SE* 22.]

37 Cf. T.W. Adorno, "How To Look at Television," *The Quarterly of Film, Radio and Television*, 8, no. 3, pp. 213ff. [Reprinted in T.W. Adorno, *The Culture Industry* (ed. J.M. Bernstein). London: Routledge, 1991.]

38 [D. Riesman, *The Lonely Crowd*. New Haven, Conn.: Yale University Press, 1950.]

39 Cf. Anna Freud, *The Ego and the Mechanisms of Defense* (New York, 1946), pp. 117ff. [London: Hogarth Press, 1948. Revised edition 1968.]

40 Cf. Max Horkheimer, "Authoritarianism and the Family Today," in *The Family: Its Function and Destiny*, ed. Anshen (New York [:Harper & Row], 1949 [reprinted 1959]).

41 [See E.H. Erikson, 'Hitler's Imagery and German Youth,' in C. Kluckhohn and H. Murray (eds), *Personality in Nature, Society and Culture*. New York: Knopf, 1948.]

42 Attention should be drawn to the analogy with the well-known antisemitic division into "good" and "bad" Jews. Cf. [T.W. Adorno *et al.*,] *The Authoritarian Personality* [New York: Harper & Row, 1950], pp. 622ff.

43 It may be mentioned in passing that the language of the column on the whole is euphemistic and that all negative aspects of life are expressed by neutral or even pleasant terms which one has to analyze pretty carefully in order to get at the reality basis. Most of the examples so far offered are at the same time examples of euphemism. The superstitious element in this device, the fear of summoning some demon by mentioning his name is well known and probably utilized. On an overt level, the fear of offending anybody plays a large role. Neither does the column want to offend the addressee by designating his weakness with its right name, nor does the addressee want to offend the higher-up even in his thoughts.

44 [In Spengler's *The Decline of the West* (2 volumes, trans. C.F. Atkinson. London: Allen & Unwin, 1926), life at the end of a cycle of history matches the 'zoölogical' condition of prehistoric life as human beings inhabit the shells of spent civilizations. Spengler attaches great importance to the city as the

icon of historical 'soul,' culture and technology. He asserts that post-historical humans dwell in cities 'as the men of the stone age sheltered in caves and pile dwellings' (vol. 2, p. 48). Adorno offers a surprisingly measured critical assessment of Spengler in his 'Spengler Today' (*Studies in Philosophy and Social Science* 9, 1941).]

45 Sigmund Freud, *Werke*, XV, "Neue Folge der Vorlesungen zur Einführung in die Psychoanalyse," p. 105. ['New Introductory Lectures on Psychoanalysis,' Lecture 32, 'Anxiety and Instinctual Life,' *SE* 22.]

2

THESES AGAINST OCCULTISM

I. The tendency to occultism is a symptom of the regression in consciousness. This has lost the power to think the unconditional and to endure the conditional. Instead of defining both, in their unity and difference, by conceptual labor, it mixes them indiscriminately. The unconditional becomes fact, the conditional an immediate essence. Monotheism is decomposing into a second mythology. "I believe in astrology, because I do not believe in God," one participant in an American socio-psychological investigation answered. Judicious reason, that had elevated itself to the notion of one God, seems ensnared in his fall. Spirit is dissociated into spirits and thereby forfeits the power to recognize that they do not exist. The veiled tendency of society towards disaster lulls its victims in a false revelation, with a hallucinated phenomenon. In vain they hope in its fragmented blatancy to look their total doom in the eye and withstand it. Panic breaks once again, after millennia of enlightenment, over a humanity whose control of nature as control of men far exceeds in horror anything men ever had to fear from nature.[1]

II. The second mythology is more untrue than the first. The first was the precipitate of the state of consciousness of successive epochs, each of which showed its consciousness to be some degrees more free of blind subservience to nature than had the previous. The former, deranged and bemused, throws away the hard-won knowledge of itself, in the midst of a society which, by the all-encompassing exchange-relationship, eliminates precisely the elemental power the occultists claim to command. The helmsman looking to the Dioscuri,[2] the attribution of animation to tree and spring, in all their deluded bafflement before the unexplained, were historically appropriate to the subject's experiences of the objects of his actions. As a rationally exploited reaction to rationalized society, however, in the booths and consulting rooms of seers of all gradations, reborn animism denies the alienation of which it is itself proof and product, and concocts surrogates for non-existent experience. The occultist draws the ultimate conclusion from the fetish-character of commodities: menacingly objectified labor assails him on all sides from demonically grimacing objects. What has been forgotten in a world congealed into products, the fact that it has been produced by men, is split off and misremembered as a being-in-itself added to that of the objects and equivalent to them. Because objects have frozen in the cold light of reason, lost their illusory animation, the social quality that now animates them is given an independent existence both natural and supernatural, a thing among things.

III. By its regression to magic under late capitalism, thought is assimilated to late capitalist forms. The asocial twilight phenomena in the margins of the system, the pathetic attempts to squint through the chinks in its walls, while revealing nothing of what is outside, illuminate all the more clearly the forces of decay within. The bent little fortune tellers, terrorizing their clients with crystal balls, are toy models of the great ones who hold the fate of mankind in their hands. Just as hostile and conspiratorial as the obscurantists of psychic research is society itself. The hypnotic power exerted by things occult resembles totalitarian terror: in present-day processes the two are merged. The smiling of auguries is amplified to society's sardonic laughter at itself, gloating over the direct material exploitation of souls. The horoscope corresponds to the official directives to the nations, and number-mysticism is preparation for administrative statistics and cartel prices. Integration itself proves in the end to be an ideology for disintegration into power groups which exterminate each other. He who integrates is lost.

IV. Occultism is a reflex-action to the subjectification of all meaning, the complement of reification. If, to the living, objective reality seems deaf as never before, they try to elicit meaning from it by saying abracadabra. Meaning is attributed indiscriminately to the next worse thing: the rationality of the real,[3] no longer quite convincing, is replaced by hopping tables and rays from heaps of earth. The offal of the pheno-menal world becomes, to sick consciousness, the *mundus intelligibilis*. It might almost be speculative truth, just as Kafka's Odradek[4] is almost an angel, and yet it is, in a positivity that excludes the medium of thought, only barbaric aberration alienated from itself, subjectivity mistaking itself for its object. The more consummate the inanity of what is fobbed off as 'spirit' – and in anything less spiritless the enlightened subject would at once recognize itself – the more the meaning detected there, which in fact is not there at all, becomes an unconscious compulsive projection of a subject decomposing historically if not clinically. It would like to make the world resemble its own decay: therefore it has dealings with requisites and evil wishes. "The third one reads out of my hand,/ She wants to read my doom!" In occultism, the mind groans under its own spell like someone in a nightmare, whose torment grows with the feeling that he is dreaming yet cannot wake up.

V. The power of occultism, as of Fascism, to which it is connected by thought patterns of the ilk of anti-Semitism, is not only pathic. Rather, it lies in the fact that in the lesser panaceas, as in superimposed pictures, consciousness famished for truth imagines it is grasping a dimly present knowledge diligently denied to it by official progress in all its forms. It is the knowledge that society, by virtually excluding the possibility of spontaneous change, is gravitating towards total catastrophe. The real absurdity is reproduced in the astrological hocus-pocus, which adduces the impenetrable connections of alienated elements – nothing more alien than the stars – as knowledge about the subject. The menace deciphered in the constellations resembles the historical threat that propagates itself precisely through unconsciousness, absence of subjects. That all are prospective victims of a whole made up solely of themselves, they can make bearable only by transferring that whole to something similar but external. In the woeful idiocy they practice, their empty horror, they are able to vent their impracticable woe, their crass fear of death, and yet continue to repress it, as they must if they wish to go on living. The break in the line of life that indicates a lurking cancer is a fraud only in the place where it purports to be found, the individual's hand; where they refrain from diagnosis, in the collective, it would be correct. Occultists rightly feel drawn towards childishly monstrous scientific fantasies. The confusion they sow between their emanations and the isotopes of uranium is ultimate clarity. The mystical rays are modest anticipations of technical ones. Superstition is knowledge, because it sees together the ciphers of destruction scattered on the social surface; it is folly because in all its death-wish it still clings to illusions: expecting from the transfigured shape of society misplaced in the skies an answer that only a study of real society can give.

VI. Occultism is the metaphysic of dunces. The mediocrity of the mediums is no more accidental than the apocryphal triviality of the revelations. Since the early days of spiritualism, the beyond has conveyed nothing more significant than the dead grandmother's greetings and the prophecy of an immanent journey. The excuse that the world of spirits can convey no more to poor human reason than the latter can take in, is equally absurd, an auxiliary hypothesis of the paranoiac system; the *lumen naturale* has, after all, taken us somewhat further than the journey to grandmother, and if the spirits do not wish to acknowledge this, they are ill-mannered hobgoblins with whom it is better to break off all dealings. The platitudinously natural content of the supernatural message betrays its untruth. In pursuing yonder what they have lost, they encounter only the nothing they have. In order not to lose touch with the everyday dreariness in which, as irremediable realists, they are at home, they adapt the meaning they revel in to the meaninglessness they flee. The worthless magic is nothing other than the worthless existence it lights up. This is what makes the prosaic so cosy. Facts which differ from what is the case only by not being facts are trumped up as a fourth dimension. Their non-being alone is their *qualitas occulta*. They supply simpletons with a world outlook. With their blunt, drastic answers to every question, the astrologists and spiritualists do not so much solve problems as remove them by crude premises from all possibility of solution. Their sublime realm, conceived as analogous to space, no more needs to be thought than chairs and flower-vases. It thus reinforces conformism. Nothing better pleases what is there than that being there should, as such, be meaning.

VII. The great religions have either, like Judaism after the ban on graven images, veiled the redemption of the dead in silence, or preached the resurrection of the flesh. They take the inseparability of the spiritual and physical seriously. For them there was no intention, nothing 'spiritual,' that was not somehow founded in bodily perception and sought bodily fulfillment. To the occultists, who consider the idea of resurrection beneath them, and actually do not want to be saved, this is too coarse. Their metaphysics, which even Huxley can no longer distinguish from Metaphysics, rests on the axiom: "The soul can soar to the heights, heigh-ho,/the body stays put on the sofa below." The heartier the spirituality, the more mechanistic: not even Descartes drew the line so cleanly. Division of labour and reification are taken to the extreme: body and soul severed in a kind of perennial vivisection. The soul is to shake the dust off its feet and in brighter regions forthwith resume its fervent activity at the exact point where it was interrupted. In this declaration of independence, however, the soul becomes a cheap imitation of that from which it had achieved a false emancipation. In place of the interaction that even the most rigid philosophy admitted, the astral body is installed, ignominious concession of hypostasized spirit to its opponent. Only in the metaphor of the body can the concept of pure spirit be grasped at all, and is at the same time cancelled. In their reification the spirits are already negated.

VIII. They inveigh against materialism. But they want to weigh the astral body. The objects of their interests are supposed at once to transcend the possibility of experience, and be experienced. Their procedure is to be strictly scientific: the greater the humbug, the more meticulously the experiment is prepared. The self importance of scientific checks is taken *ad absurdum* where there is nothing to check. The same rationalistic and empiricist apparatus that threw the spirits out is being used to reimpose them on those who no longer trust their own reason. As if any elemental spirit would not turn tail for the traps that domination of nature sets for such fleeting beings. But even this the occultists turn to advantage. Because the spirits do not like controls, in the midst of all the safety precautions a tiny door must be left open, through which they can make their unimpeded entrance. For occultists are practical folk. Not driven by vain curiosity, they are looking for tips. From the stars to forward transactions is but a nimble step. Usually the information amounts to no more than that some poor acquaintance has had his dearest hopes dashed.

IX. The cardinal sin of occultism is the contamination of mind and existence, the latter becoming itself an attribute of mind. Mind arose out of existence, as an organ for keeping alive. In reflecting existence, however, it becomes at the same time something else. The existent negates itself as thought upon itself. Such negation is mind's element. To attribute to it positive existence, even of a higher order, would be to deliver it up to what it opposes. Late bourgeois ideology has again made it what it was for pre-animism, a being-in-itself modeled on the social division of labour, on the split between manual and intellectual labor, on the planned domination over the former. In the concept of mind-in-itself, consciousness has ontologically justified and perpetuated privilege by making it independent of the social principle by which it is constituted. Such ideology explodes in occultism: it is Idealism come full circle. Just by virtue of the rigid antithesis of being and mind, the latter becomes a department of being. If Idealism demanded solely on behalf of the whole, the Idea, that being be mind and that the latter exist, occultism draws the absurd conclusion that existence is determinate being:

> Existence, after it has become, is always being with a non-being, so that this non-being is taken up in simple unity with the being. Non-being taken up in being, the fact that the concrete whole is in the form of being, of immediacy, constitutes determinateness as such. [5]

The occultists take literally the non-being as in 'simple unity with being',

and their kind of concreteness is a surreptitious short-cut from the whole
to the determinate which can defend itself by claiming that the whole,
having once been determined, is no longer the whole. They call to
metaphysics: *Hic Rhodus hic salta*:[6] if the philosophic investment of spirit
with existence is determinable, then finally, they sense, any scattered
piece of existence must be justifiable as a particular spirit. The doctrine
of the existence of the spirit, the ultimate exaltation of bourgeois consciousness, consequently bore teleologically within it the belief in spirits,
its ultimate degradation. The shift to existence, always 'positive' and
justifying the world, implies at the same time the thesis of the positivity
of mind, pinning it down, transposing the absolute into appearance.
Whether the whole objective world as 'product,' is to be spirit, or a
particular thing a particular spirit, ceases to matter, and the world-spirit
becomes the supreme Spirit, the guardian angel of the established,
de-spiritualized order. On this the occultists live: their mysticism is the
enfant terrible of the mystical moment in Hegel. They take speculation to
the point of fraudulent bankruptcy. In passing off determinate being as
mind, they put objectified mind to the test of existence, which must
prove negative. No spirit exists.[7]

NOTES

*The editor's notes, or editorial additions to Adorno's notes, are enclosed in square
brackets.*

1 [This passage re-states the basic thesis of *Dialectic of Enlightenment*. The
enlightenment project to install human control over nature as a way of
warding-off the fear of nature has the ultimate effect of engendering an even
greater fear of the products of human technology.]

2 [The mythological twins Castor and Pollux, associated with the constellation
Gemini and with the double form of St Elmo's fire, regarded by sailors as a
lucky omen.]

3 [An allusion to Hegel's metaphysics. As Adorno goes on to write,
"Occultism is the metaphysic of dunces." The thrust of the rather dense
paragraph IX below, which turns on a quotation from Hegel's *Logic*, is that
occultism is both a crass vulgarization of "high" bourgeois metaphysics and
at the same time a clue to the kernel of postivistic fatuity that lurks at the
heart of metaphysics and makes its degeneration inevitable.]

4 [The Odradek features in Kafka's *Die Sorge des Hausvaters* (translated as "The
Cares of a Family Man" in F. Kafka, *The Penal Colony: Stories and Short Pieces*.
New York: Schocken Books, 1961). Looking like a "star shaped spool for
thread" the immortal Odradek, while of "no fixed abode," appears and
disappears around the house.]

5 G.W.F. Hegel, *Wissenschaft der Logik*, *Werke* 5, p. 116 (*Hegel's Science of Logic*
[trans. A.V. Miller]. London [:George Allen & Unwin], 1969, p. 110).

6 ["Here is Rhodes, jump here," the ripost in a fable of Aesop's to the man who claims to be able to jump over Rhodes. It is Hegel's quotation of the saying which gives it its point for Adorno here. Hegel writes immediately afterwards

> It is just as absurd to fancy that a philosophy can transcend its contemporary age as it is to fancy that an individual can leap over his own age, jump over Rhodes. If his theory goes beyond the world as it is and builds an ideal one as it ought to be, that world exists indeed, but only in his opinions, an unsubstantial element where anything you please may, in fancy, be built.
>
> (*Hegel's Philosophy of Right* (trans. T.M. Knox). Oxford: Oxford University Press, 1952, p. 11).

So, occultism calls the bluff of (Hegelian) metaphysics by taking literally, or positivistically, its prohibition on the speculative transcendence of "what is." However, this literalism recapitulates the error as occultism builds anything it pleases in the para-material 'spirit-world.']

7 ["*Kein Geist is da*" (T.W. Adorno, *Minima Moralia*. Frankfurt: Suhrkamp Verlag, 1978, p. 329). Perhaps "no spirit is there," or "there is no spirit." Jephcott's translation has the virtue of underlining a major point of this paragraph: that it is a crude and consequential positivistic error to endow *Geist* with the kind of "existence" enjoyed by material objects. A further difficulty is the notorious ambiguity of the German *Geist*, which is both "mind" and "spirit." This double meaning helps Adorno to move between the "spirits" of occultism and the "mind" of Hegelian metaphysics. At one point he uses the word "spirit" – *Obersten Spirit*, "supreme Spirit."]

3

RESEARCH PROJECT ON ANTI-SEMITISM: IDEA OF THE PROJECT

A. SPECIFIC CHARACTER OF THE PROJECT

Propaganda to combat anti-Semitism has often been crude and ineffective because of a lack of knowledge of its psychological roots, individual as well as social. In spite of the many excellent works written on the subject, anti-Semitism is still regarded too casually and viewed too superficially, even by those whom it immediately affects. For too many people anti-Semitism is nothing more than a pitiable aberration, a relapse into the Dark Ages; and while its presence is understandable in those nations of middle and Eastern Europe whose post-war status made the permanent achievement of democracy impossible, it is on the whole viewed as an element foreign to the spirit of modern society. From this point of view, it would follow logically that anti-Semitism is an anachronism, incapable of securing a world-wide hold. This is not true. Hatred of the Jews, despite the proclamation of human rights during the most progressive periods and in the most progressive countries, has never really been vanquished and is capable of flaring up anew at any moment.

The purpose of this project is to show that anti-Semitism is one of the dangers inherent in all more recent culture. The project will combine historical, psychological, and economic research with experimental studies. Several new hypotheses will be presented which are the result of former studies of the Institute, such as that progressive modern thought has an ambivalent attitude toward the concept of human rights, that the persecution of the aristocrats in the French Revolution bears a resemblance to anti-Semitism in modern Germany, that the foreign rather than the German masses are the spectators for whom German pogroms are arranged, and so forth.

More concretely, the project will analyze the representative thought of more recent European literature and of specific historical events in order to reveal the deep roots of anti-Semitism, and a series of experiments will reveal the characteristic features of anti-Semitism in order to make it more easily recognizable in countries where it is now largely latent.

A weighty objection might be raised against a thorough scientific treatment of anti-Semitism. In dealing with the deeper mechanisms of anti-Semitism one cannot avoid mentioning things which will not be entirely agreeable to Jews. We are thinking especially of our subsection on the so-called character traits of the Jews and the genesis of these traits. One might raise the issue that anti-Semitic propagandists could misuse this and other results of our research.

We do not share this point of view. The fear that truth can also be put to bad use should never paralyze the energy needed to uncover it in its entirety, especially in such vital problems. The growing custom of suppressing important elements of the truth for so-called tactical reasons is taking on more and more dangerous traits. It easily leads to an optimism which is satisfied to bask in general concepts such as the rights of man, progress, enlightenment, etc., without realizing that in the present phase of society these concepts tend to become mere phrases, just as the fascist advocates of persecution cynically charge.

Furthermore, it is exceedingly important for the struggle against anti-Semitism that those Jewish and non-Jewish progressive circles, which even today close their eyes to the gravity of the problem, become stirred by a scientific demonstration of its underlying causes. They must be freed from the erroneous belief that anti-Semitism exists only where it is openly expressed, for it finds nooks even in the hearts of the noblest of humans. To activate the Jews who feel reassured by the sincere protests against the German pogroms uttered by many important personalities in this and other countries, it is less important to analyze the statements of Julius Streicher than the correspondence of Voltaire and other philosophers of the Enlightenment. As long as anti-Semitism exists as a constant undercurrent in social life, its influence reaches all groups of the population and it can always be rekindled by suitable propaganda.

B. DIVISION OF THE PROJECT

Section I Current theories about anti-Semitism

The traditional theories about anti-Semitism, of which but a few will be mentioned here, fall roughly into two groups: the rationalistic and the anti-Semitic.

(a) Among the rationalistic theses, the following deserve special mention:

(1) "There is in fact no anti-Semitism at all." That is, there are no real psychological reactions which could be regarded as primarily anti-Semitic. All anti-Semitism is artificially made up and propagated as a manoeuvre for mass betrayal, or for the sake of distraction or robbery. The anti-Semitic reactions of the masses have merely been invented. In essence, this theory is most closely related to the idea held by many enlighteners who denounced religion as a mere "hoax of the clergy." In our view, it is much too superficial. It overlooks the fact that the actual anti-Semitic reactions themselves fulfill a decided social and psychological function. In the struggle against anti-Semitism we cannot content ourselves solely with unmasking it as a mere ideology, but must get at the roots of those of its elements which are genuine. Among these, the apparently irrational ones, the idiosyncrasies, are preeminent.

(2) The apologetic thesis that all the objections to the Jew raised by anti-Semites are frame-ups and lies – a thesis closely related to the one above. The discrediting of cheap apologetics is of central importance in the project. It is necessary to analyze the alleged qualities of the Jew which elicit anti-Semitism in order to discover which of them have a basis in reality and which are invented. The "inferiority" which is most frequently mentioned in this connection today[1] is an illustration of the former category although not the most important. The qualities to which anti-Semites constantly refer with apparent justification cannot be understood as natural constants, as eternal biological laws; they must be regarded as character traits that may disappear along with the conditions which gave rise to them, as their disappearance in some countries already indicates.

(3) The formal sociological thesis reduces hatred for the Jews and for their specific qualities to the general category of strangeness.[2] It assumes the national cohesion of the Jews and a tenacious adherence on their part to their religion. This thesis, like the preceding ones, is just one side of the truth, particularly applicable to older features of anti-Semitism.

(4) The theory of envy holds that anti-Semitism is rooted in the superior intelligence and efficiency of the Jews. Because of their outstanding qualities the Jews achieve high positions in every field, thus provoking the resentment of the materially and psychologically handicapped. This thesis is too rationalistic, psychologically speaking. It assumes that anti-Semitism is caused by entirely conscious experiences and considerations, whereas such considerations actually play a relatively small part. The element of envy is of some importance, in a shifted or perverted form (e.g. the supposition of the physical psychological, and

social inferiority of the Jews) rather than in a direct form. More details concerning the conscious and subconscious envy of the Jews will be developed in the typological section.

(5) Anti-Semitism is the "socialism of fools." This theory was brought forward by social democrats (Bebel). It implies that the lower middle class in rural and metropolitan areas regards the destruction of its Jewish creditor and competitor as the easiest way out of its economic distress. This economic interpretation contains some truth, too, but it must be supplemented by an analysis of the psychological mechanisms which make even those sections of the masses which are not at all dependent on Jewish business particularly susceptible to anti-Semitic propaganda.

(b) Finally, there are the actually anti-Semitic theories, particularly the thesis that Jews are by nature extreme revolutionists and have provided a large number of the leaders of the labor movement. The degree of truth in this view can be checked only by a careful comparison of the histories and social conditions of different countries. A similar analysis is to be made of the parallel thesis that the Jews are extremely capitalistic. Sombart's work, which took on a slight pro-Semitic veneer, has furthered this view considerably. He even hinted at the National Socialist equation, democratic-liberalistic-capitalistic, as well as at the myth of the power of Jewish money.

Section II Anti-Semitism and mass movements

This section is not intended as a history of anti-Semitism. Its aim is to reveal, by selected historical events, a set of socio-psychological trends which are characteristic of anti-Semitism as a whole. These trends are not manifested exclusively in anti-Semitic outbreaks; their basic structure can be seen in activities which have been conducted against other social groups as well. The recurrence of punishment and destruction throughout more recent history throws some light upon destructive character traits which remained latent in broad sections of the population even during "quiet" periods. It is generally overlooked that present-day National Socialism contains potentialities which have been dormant not only in Germany but also in many other parts of the world. Many phenomena familiar in totalitarian countries (for instance, the role of the leader, mass meetings, fraternizing, drunken enthusiasm, the myth of sacrifice, the contempt of the individual, etc.) can be understood only historically – that is, from the foundations of the whole of modern history. In this section, relatively well known facts will be treated by contrasting them anew with descriptions of current problems of anti-Semitism, and socio-psychological mechanisms that are still effective will be analyzed.

(a) The First Crusade.

The popular leaders under whom massacres were committed generally display ascetic features. One has only to think of Peter of Amiens, the priests Gottschalk and Volkmer, and of other preachers. The role of short slogans is also characteristic. At that time the cry, "God wills it," seized literally all Europe (cf. the cry of the National Socialists, "Germany awake!"). The masses followed that slogan, feeling themselves part of a mystic community and filled with the certainty of forgiveness for their sins. Staking one's individual life and happiness mattered little (cf. the National Socialist doctrine of the unimportance of the individual and the pillorizing of egoism). Everyone subordinated himself to a "great idea." The annihilation of the inhabitants of whole provinces by enthusiastic Crusaders was fortified by the assertion that the action was directed against the foes of the highest leader, quite similar to the purges of the National Socialists. The unbelievers included not only the Turks and the Saracens but also the Jews and others whom the masses could overwhelm and pillage. Something which allegedly has languished for a long period must always be freed in order to serve as rationalization for the fury which explodes in such actions – either the holy sepulchre under the thumb of the heathen, or Germany under the Versailles treaty. The mass psychological significance of such ideologies will be explained.

(b) The Albigensian Crusade

In the Crusade against the Albigenses, a clergyman leader, Arnold of Citeaux, again held first rank. No distinction was made between Christian heretics and Jews. Both were struck by the same fury. The war was an attempt by the old bureaucracy of the church, which was being reorganized, to suppress the rising bourgeoisie. (Similarly, from the inception of National Socialism to the first years of its rule, 1927–1931, the old powers, Junkers, sections of the officer corps, Protestant clergymen, civil servants, and bankrupt munitions industrialists had reorganized themselves against the young democratic republic.) The political character of the war against the Albigenses also manifests itself in the fact that belief did not matter much to the Knights of the Crusade. Many Catholics were killed along with Protestants and Jews. They too belonged to the South, progressive in commerce and crafts. Unconcern about differences in ideology is characteristic of such uprisings. It reveals the fact that the fight against heresies or criminal elements is only a pretext for more underlying economic and socio-psychological tendencies.

(c) Jew-baiting in twelfth- and thirteenth-century England

During the Crusades and the first war against the Albigenses, pogroms spread over Germany, France and the East. In England, Richard the Lion-Heart originally showed no anti-Semitic tendencies; he actually protected the Jews. But popular clergymen, especially the Archbishops of Canterbury, Thomas a Becket and Baldwin, made their appearance as anti-Semitic mass leaders. The people knelt before Thomas a Becket and were gripped by collective infatuation (cf. intoxicated enthusiasm in modern mass meetings). The connection between a special type of leader cult, mass fraternizing, and pogroms is one of the most important socio-psychological subjects for investigation. In England, which was touched by the anti-Semitic wave a hundred years later than the Continent, the cool-headedness and resistance shown at first by the British Islanders did not impair the mechanisms which impel anti-Semitism. The Channel was no barrier against social contagion.

(d) The Reformation

During the time of the Reformation the Jews were not persecuted along with the heretics, as they were during the war against the Albigenses, but with the Catholics. Just as monks and nuns were accused of hoarding secret treasures in their cloisters and indulging in unnatural practices, the Jews were blamed for lurid secret crimes in addition to their superstitious rites (cf. the present accusations in Germany against Jewish Lodges and charges of vice against Catholic clergymen). The repressed drives of the population, diverted by reformers into internal discipline and fear of conscience, came forth in the inventions about Catholics and Jews.

There were young people who, leading their elders, forced their way into churches and monasteries, destroyed works of art and made fun of priests during their sermons. Again it was chiefly young people who delighted in caricatures of Jews (cf. the role of youth in the so-called years of struggle for National Socialism).

In Martin Luther the anti-Semitic arsenal is fully equipped. The anti-rationalist Luther compares reason with a wild beast and with a whore, and lumps Jews together with prostitutes.[3] Hitler forbids discussions between National Socialists and members of the other race; Luther said, "Don't dispute much with Jews about the articles of our faith."[4] Luther wanted the Jews out of Germany.

Country and streets are open to them so they might move to the country if they like. We'll give them gifts, with pleasure, in order to get rid of them because they are a heavy burden, like a plague, pestilence and misfortune in our country.[5]

His concrete suggestions, however, do not advocate presenting them with gifts and letting them go. This is how they go:

and take away from them all their cash and jewels of silver and gold, and set it apart, to be guarded.[6]

That into the hands of the young strong Jews and Jewesses are placed flails, axes, mattocks, trowels, distaffs and spindles, and they are made to earn their daily bread by the sweat of their brows [Luther says literally 'of their noses'] as it is put upon the shoulders of the children of Adam.[7]

That their synagogues or schools be set on fire.[8]

That their houses be broken up and destroyed . . . they be put under a roof or stable, like the Gypsies, in order to let them know that they are no longer masters in our country as they flatter themselves, but in misery and captivity as they incessantly lament and complain to God about us.[9]

That their right of escort on the streets be altogether abolished. For they have nothing to do in the country because they are neither knights nor officials nor merchants, nor anything of that sort, and they ought to stay at home.[10]

(e) The French Revolution

Sociological trends can be found in the French Revolution which are similar to those in popular uprisings that have an anti-Semitic flavor. Anti-Semitism is pushed into the background by the specifically equalitarian ideology. The objects of the terror are the aristocrats who, significantly enough, are branded as a race. Legislative measures, agitation, and popular uprisings against the aristocracy bear comparison to the racial upheavals of our time. There are a number of accusations against the aristocrats which correspond to the usual charges against the Jews – shirking work, parasitic character, luxury, viciousness, international connections, their claim to be chosen, etc. Similar techniques can be found in mass meetings of the French Revolution and of the present time – speeches of the leaders, the power of the sub-leaders in the provinces, fear of spies and traitors, corruption scandals, the practice of denunciation, allegedly spontaneous mass action, hatred of bank capital, hatred of foreigners, and new heathen cults. Despite their diametrically opposite aims, National Socialism has more in common with the French Revolution than is generally assumed.

(f) Wars of German Independence and other German uprisings

In the wars of German Independence in 1813–1915 and in the ensuing uprisings, several features of National Socialism are heralded. The eagerness of the free cities and of the German principalities to revoke the emancipation achieved during Napoleonic rule corresponds to the National Socialist passion to avenge the "fourteen years of disgrace," that is, the Weimar Republic in which the Jews actually possessed full civil rights. In the emancipation movements of the German bourgeoisie the universities combined anti-Semitism with the German ideology of freedom. The close relation between German Protestantism, Germanic paganism, community socialism, and German ideals of unitarian government becomes obvious. Burning of books appeared in this period. Books designated by the so-called democratic papers as unpatriotic (e.g. The *Code Napoléon*), and writings of Jewish authors were cast into the flames with the cry, "Woe to the Jews." In Würzburg, Karlsruhe, Heidelberg, Darmstadt, and Frankfurt, Jewish houses were branded and the inhabitants mistreated. All this occurred under liberal and patriotic slogans.

The movement of the "awakening" people is also found in Holland and Scandinavia. Metternich and the conservative governments had to take strong measures against the allegedly democratic masses. The farthest seeing German thinkers, for instance Goethe, Schelling and Hegel, stood against the "liberals" and on the side of the "reactionaries."

Section III Anti-Semitism in modern humanism

During the so-called enlightened era of the last 200 years, no stratum of the population has been free from anti-Semitism.

Some statements of an anti-Semitic nature can be found even in the works championing tolerance and humanism. It is important to investigate whether the passages dealing with the Jews disclose an ambivalence toward the concept of universal love for man, despite the fact that the authors present that concept quite sincerely. It is also important to investigate the relevance of the less exposed portions of the works of most writers who "stuck up for" the Jews. We must finally find out whether in an unguarded moment they betrayed the fact that their pro-Semitism did not overcome a deep feeling of alienation.

Proof that such contradictions exist within the individual in modern society would be particularly important for the evaluation of the many indignant declarations against anti-Semitism. Such declarations are dangerous in that they might easily lead to the erroneous belief that anti-Semitism has disappeared, at least among educated people.

The contradictions which may be found even with the most sincere proponents of the humanitarian ideal could throw light on the status of the reactionary and uneducated sections of the population. If ambivalence is present in the most progressive personalities, it will be all the sharper in the less cultured and enlightened individuals. Some scattered examples follow in the hope that they make clear what is meant by these contradictions in the works of great thinkers.

(a) French Enlightenment

Voltaire: His name is a symbol of philosophical enlightenment and bourgeois freedom. He, more than any of his contemporaries, recognized the sufferings of the Jews and the injustices inflicted upon them. His attacks upon the Biblical history of the Jewish people are actually directed against the Christian Church belief. The Old Testament was a somewhat vulnerable point in the Church dogma because, unlike the wonders of the New Testament, it was not well protected by the authority of the Church and removed from profane thinking, but was left largely to the mercy of profane thinking; at the same time it plays its role in the canon of the Holy Writ, and the disenchantment of the Old Testament's wonders throws its light indirectly on those of the New. One can say that Voltaire's attacks against the Old Testament, insofar as they are not really directed at the Jews but indirectly against the Christian dogma which hindered the emancipation of the Jews, benefited the latter indirectly. Nevertheless, perhaps not even Voltaire was free from anti-Semitic prejudice. In the *Essais sur les mœurs* (chapter 103)[11] he says that one is

amazed at the hatred and contempt which all nations have continually shown toward the Jews; this attitude is the necessary outcome of the Jewish law. Either they must subdue everything, or they must be thrown into the dust themselves . . . Later, when their eyes were opened a little more by victor nations, who taught them that the world was larger than they believed, their law itself made them natural fools of these nations, and finally of the whole human race.

"I know," he says in a letter,

143

that some Jews live in the English colonies. These crooks go wherever money can be made, like the Parsees, the Banians, and the Armenians . . . But if these circumcised Israelites who sell old trousers to the savages, trace themselves back to the tribes of Naphtalimuch or Issachar, it does not make any difference. Anyhow, they are the greatest scoundrels who have ever besmirched the face of the earth.[12]

(b) German Philosophy

Herder: He is the author of *The Letters for the Promulgation of Humanism*. Consciously he always advocated humanitarianism and justice. His glorification of Hebrew poetry seems to protect him from any suspicion of anti-Semitism. But there are passages which might lead us to believe that there also exists a totally different Herder. He says in *Adastraea*,V. 7 (Conversion of the Jews)[13] that Luther's utterances about the Jews were often too callous, in accordance with his time.

> They have since been reaffirmed to such a degree that around the end of the last century, when some Jewish fathers of the family tried conditionally to associate and affiliate themselves to a newly built and enlightened Christendom, no one paid much attention to them.

He does not consider it reasonable to talk too much about human rights when faced with the concrete issues of the Jewish problem:

> As the business of the Jews has been known for more than three thousand years, the influence which it has had and immutably still has upon the character of that people shows itself throughout their history. Why then those more distant, far-fetched discussions, for instance, about the rights of humanity, if the question is only this: How many of this foreign people shall be allowed to conduct *this, their business*, in this European state, without detriment to the natives? Under what conditions? With what limitations? Under whose supervision? For, unfortunately, history provides sad proof that an unlimited number of them corrupt a European state, particularly one which is badly organized. Not general *humanitarian principles*, but the constitution of the nation in which the Jews carry on their profession, answers these questions.

Herder expressly polemicizes against other countries patterning their attitude on the treatment of the Jews in Holland, at that time a progressive country.

Kant: According to Kant, it is an unconditional task to regard every man not as a means but as an end. By "end" Kant refers to man's position of esteem because he is a free, autonomous, rational being. His remarks about the Jews, however, do not seem at all in accord with his postulate of practical reason. The contradiction to his universal principle of morals is evident; it is hopeless to improve the Jews.

> The Palestinians living among us, even the bulk of them, have earned the not unfounded reputation of cheats because of their usurious minds. It seems strange to think of a nation of cheats. But it is just as strange to think of a nation of merchants . . . acknowledged by the state, who not receiving any civic honor, desire to compensate for their loss, by outwitting the people under whose protection they live, and even each other . . . Instead of the futile plan to "moralize" this people with regard to fraud and honesty, I'd rather like to profess my hypothesis . . . about that odd status.[14]

Fichte: Fichte's theories of freedom, and later, of socialism, have, rightly or wrongly, been enthusiastically accepted by many European liberals and Socialists. His moral rigorism, which, like Kant's, urges that man be judged not according to natural (i.e., racial) criteria but according to his fulfillment of duty, nevertheless condemned the Jews:

> Throughout almost all European countries, a mighty, hostile state is expanding. It is constantly at war with them, and in some countries it weighs horribly upon the inhabitants. I don't believe that Jewry has become so terrible because it constitutes a separate and tightly chained state of its own . . . but because this state is based upon the hatred of the entire human race . . . Does not the reasonable thought occur to you here that the Jews, who have a state of their own without you will grind you other inhabitants under their heels as soon as you give them civic rights?

He comments upon these remarks in the footnote: "Let the poisoned breath of intolerance be far from these pages, as it is from my heart." And yet, "To give civic rights to the Jews, I see no measure but cutting off all their heads, and replacing them by other heads in which there is not a single Jewish idea left. To protect us from them, again, I see no other means but to conquer their Promised Land for them in order to send them there altogether."[15]

Hegel: Hegel is distinguished from most philosophers of his time by his insight into the world historical situation. He showed only contempt for the Teutonic and anti-Semitic currents in the German universities. He staunchly advocated the granting of civic rights to the Jews. Some statements can be found which might contain hints of hatred for Jews:

> The great tragedy of the Jewish people . . . can only create disgust . . . The fate of the Jewish people is the fate of Macbeth who overstepped the boundaries of Nature itself, clung to hetero-geneous, weird beings, trod upon and murdered in their service everything that is sacred to human nature, was abandoned by his gods (for they were objects and he was a slave), and finally was smitten as a consequence of his own belief.
>
> The Jewish people have been driven to Hell in the infamy of their hatred. Whoever of them has been left stalking the earth has remained as a memento.[16]

According to Hegel's philosophy one can say about the Jewish people "that just because they were at the threshold of salvation, they are and have been the most object of all."[17]

Goethe: Goethe was no anti-Semite. On the contrary, there are many highly positive remarks in his writings about the qualities of the Jews, about their practical minds, their perseverence and tenacity. Anti-Semitic sentences are not phrased directly, but as opinions of poetic characters, whom, however, he frequently draws with sympathy. Characteristic of the time in which Goethe lived is the way in which he associates Jews and Catholic priests:[18] "Cowls for magicians, Jews and sky-pilots." They "wrangled over whether he was a sky-pilot or a Jew." Mephistopheles says, "The Church alone, be it confessed, Daughters, can ill-got wealth digest." And Faust remarks, "It is a general custom, too, Practiced alike by king and Jew."[19] In *Wilhelm Meister's Wanderjahre* the principles of a Utopian community are described. One passage reads: We do not tolerate "any Jews among us, for how could we grant them participation in the highest culture, whose origin and descent they deny?" (Book III, Chapter XI). Goethe writes in the *Swiss Journey*:[20] "The people there are thoroughly polite, and in their behavior show a good natural, quiet burgher way of thinking. Jews are not tolerated there."

Such an analysis lies at the bottom of Treitschke's judgment of anti-Semitism throughout the history of the German mind. "From Luther on down to Goethe, Herder, Kant and Fichte, almost all great Germanic thinkers agreed in this feeling. Lessing, with his predilection for the Jews, was quite singular."[21] The only one among the later writers who resembled Lessing in this respect was Nietzsche. (We do not give any examples of pro-Semitic statements here. In the study itself we shall deal extensively with Nietzsche's positive attitude toward the Jews.)

Such inconsistency as may exist between the concrete utterances about the Jews and the humanitarian ideal within individuals would be only part of the universal contradiction between the dire reality of modern society and the dream of harmony among all humanity. The latter was consciously proclaimed by all the above thinkers. They devoted all the spiritual powers at their disposal to it. They were rooted, however, in the reality of their environment; their impulses, their intimate sympathies, and aversions derived therefrom.

(d) French Novel

No matter how energetically Zola, the defender of Captain Dreyfuss, fought against hatred of the Jews, elements can be found in his own works which could be classed as identical with official anti-Semitism. In his novel, *L' Argent*, Zola pictures a Jew of whom he says,

> The public wealth was devoured by the ever increasing fortune of a single individual. Gundermann (the Jew in question) was, in fact, the master, the almighty king. Paris and the whole world lay trembling and obedient at his feet.

Fantastic conceptions about Jewish riches and power, about the coldness and calculation of the Jews, keep recurring in French literature since Balzac.

Our analyses of these anti-Semitic tendencies of philosophers and writers are not undertaken in order to blame them for subjective insincerity. Our purpose is rather, through the revelation of these unconscious and hidden germs of anti-Semitism, to expose the problem in all its seriousness.

Section IV Types of present-day anti-Semites

Much of the misunderstanding about anti-Semitism has its roots in the confusion of its very different types. The success of any attempt to fight anti-Semitism depends largely on knowledge of the social and psychological genesis of its various species, often indiscernible in daily life. The types of anti-Semites are here considered from both the historical and psychological points of view.

We believe ourselves safe from the misunderstanding that according to this typology (in which even the pro-Semites are mentioned) all

Christians are anti-Semites. The classification does not intend to distribute large groups of individuals among these types, but merely to formulate with theoretical precision a number of extreme possibilities of anti-Semitic attitudes. Neither do we claim that any individual who shows any of the character traits mentioned in the typology is an anti-Semite merely because of those traits, nor do we even assert that actual anti-Semites can be classified entirely according to the principles indicated. In reality the anti-Semites will often appear as combinations and intermediate forms of the "ideal possibilities" mentioned here.

(a) The "born" anti-Semite

The basic quality of this type is the renunciation of rational justification. He reacts with apparent "instinct" against so-called Jewish racial traits – flat feet, smell, hooked nose, Jewish accent, gesticulation, etc. His nausea is a reaction to the scars of mutilation which history has stamped upon the Jews. Even their names (Itzig, Levy, Cohn) are repugnant to him. He simply cannot stand the Jews. It can often be observed that this type appreciates so called "racy" women akin to the Jewish type if they are presented to him as Gentile (note the success of Pola Negri with the National Socialists). This trend indicates that the allegedly natural anti-Semitism in some of its representatives is actually an over-compensation for suppressed or inhibited desires.

(b) The religious-philosophical anti-Semite

Although this type has largely disappeared, there are still a good many left who regard the Jews as adherents of a hostile religion. The Jews have crucified Christ. They have remained impenitent for thousands of years. They particularly ought to have been summoned to recognize him since they were witnesses of his activity and of his passion, but they have persisted in denying him. Hence the Jewish religion is in effect equivalent to absolute disbelief. The Jew is Judas. He is the stranger who deliberately excludes himself from the Christian community. He can compensate for his guilt by baptism, but even then he deserves distrust until he can prove that he has seriously atoned. Many non-believing Christians resent the Jew's tenacious adherence to outdated superstitious rites. They feel that he should have joined the dominant religion, for social and humanitarian if not for religious reasons. This category includes many humanists, Goethe, Schopenhauer, and Hegel, insofar as they attach reservations to their favorable comments on Jews.

(c) The back-woods or sectarian anti-Semite

This type has made anti-Semitism a substitute for religion, as other groups have vegetarianism, Krishna Murti, or any other physical or psychical panacea. The imaginary world of the sectarian anti-Semite is dominated by the notion of conspiracy. He believes in Jewish world domination; he swears by the Elders of Zion. On the other hand, he himself tends to favor conspiracies which have much in common, structurally, with the images he fears (Ku Klux Klan, etc.). He considers Freemasonry and other fraternal orders to be the greatest of world perils, but he himself founds lodge-like congregations whenever possible. He has the reverence of the semi-erudite for science and believes that non-intercourse with Jews is a sort of natural cure for rejuvenating man and world.

(d) The vanquished competitor

The place of this type in the processes of production necessarily brings him into conflict with the Jews. He comes from the lower strata who are compelled to buy from Jews and to fall into their debt, from among the owners of specialty shops who are forced out of business by the competition of Jewish owned department stores, etc. His hatred does not stem from specific characteristics of the Jews but rather from certain economic relationships through which he suffers.

Since this type of anti-Semitism has some basis in reality, it also has a certain rational character. Under certain conditions therefore, it can disappear easily. For example, during the last few years in Germany, National Socialism has, to a great extent, been deserted by these people (innkeepers, provision dealers, peasants, etc.). The promised improvement of conditions by anti-Semitic measures did not materialize. Therefore, these groups have abandoned anti-Semitism as a panacea.

(e) The well-bred anti-Semite

This is the anti-Semitism of the upper bourgeois strata who want to emulate the exclusiveness of the aristocrats which was formerly directed against them. This type of anti-Semitism, prevalent in all nations, is particularly common in the Anglo-Saxon world. Whatever may be the elements of truth in the reason usually adduced by its representatives (for instance the failure of some groups of immigrants to assimilate themselves to their new surroundings), the attitude as a whole is a phenomenon of imitation, similar to fox-hunts, chateau-like country estates, etc. Rationalizations are manifold. In addition to the religious and political arguments, those aimed at Jewish manners are particularly numerous. The Jews are supposed to be loud, unreserved, obtrusive; their inferiority complex necessitates their pushing themselves into the foreground; they are grumbling and querulous; they want the best for the least money. One always has unfortunate experiences with them. Jewish intellectuals are as impossible as Jewish business men. Their intellectual conversations break the rules of the game. They resemble shop talk. Anyone whose emotions are too easily stirred is ignoble. Here the proverbial exception actually has the function of proving the rule.

(f) The "Condottiere" anti-Semite

This type has arisen with the increased insecurity of post–war existence. He is convinced that what matters is not life but chance. He is nihilistic, not out of a "drive for destruction" but because he is indifferent to individual existence. One of the reservoirs out of which this type arises is the modern unemployed. He differs from former unemployed in that his contact with the sphere of production is sporadic, if any. Individuals belonging to his category can no longer expect to be regularly absorbed by the labor process. From their youth they have been ready to act wherever they could grab something. They are inclined to hate the Jew partly because of his cautiousness and physical inefficacy, partly because, being themselves unemployed, they are economically uprooted, unusually susceptible to any propaganda, and ready to follow any leader. The other reservoir, at the opposite pole of society, is the group belonging to the dangerous professions, colonial adventures, racing motorists, airplane aces. They are the born leaders of the former group. Their ideal, actually an heroic one, is all the more sensitive to the "destructive," critical intellect of the Jews because they themselves are not quite convinced of their ideal in the depths of their hearts, but have developed it as a rationalization of their dangerous way of living. The anti-Semitic tendencies within certain groups of the German youth movement follow the same direction.

G. The "Jew-baiter"

All types are potentially sadistic. Here, however, anti–Semitism is a relatively thin pretext for repressed fury. This type hates the alleged weakness of humanitarianism, which he brands as cowardice, and which he characterizes as *Duselei* (somnolence or reverie). What he hates most of all is the Jew's allegedly higher psychological faculty for "enjoying life."

This type hates the revolutionary Jew because he "wants to have it better." Nevertheless, he is himself pseudo-revolutionary, insofar as his fury is basically the naked drive for destruction, although that drive realizes itself only in excesses allowed from above. Hence he calls his own counter-revolutionary addiction to action, revolution, and the revolution, Capitalism. Many of the more radical people liquidated by Hitler in his purges and a large number of the present SS leaders fall in this category. The relation of this type of anti-Semitism to sexual drives, which incidentally has much in common with the earlier *Radauantisemitismus* (rowdy anti-Semitism), is comparatively unconcealed. It is often based upon unconscious or conscious homosexuality.

(h) The fascist-political anti-Semite

This type is characterized by sober intelligence. He is cold, without affections, and is perhaps the most merciless of all. He deals with anti-Semitism as an export article. He has no immediate gratification from the persecution of the Jews, and if he has, it is only incidental. He deliberately plans their annihilation. He fulfills his task by administrative measures without any personal contact with the victims. He does not have to hate the Jews; he is able to negotiate with foreign ones most amiably. To him anti-Semitism is reified. It must function. He organizes the "spontaneous" actions of the people against the Jews. He holds in contempt the henchmen of his own will, perhaps even more than the Jews. He is nihilistic, too, but in a cynical way. "The Jewish question will be solved strictly legally," is the way he talks about the cold pogrom. Whereas Streicher is representative of the Jew baiter, Goebbels is the incarnation of the fascist-political anti-Semite. The tremendous propaganda value of anti-Semitism throughout the world may be the only reason the fascist leaders keep anti-Semitism alive.

(i) The Jew-lover

Those persons are really free of anti-Semitism to whom the distinction makes no difference, to whom the so-called racial traits appear unessential. There are people, however, who stress the differences between Jews and Christians in a way friendly to the Jews. This type of thinking contains an anti-Semitic nucleus which has its origin in racial discrimination. The Jews are exceedingly sensitive to this kind of anti-Semitism. The declaration of a man who professes to be particularly fond of the Jews because of their "prophetic" or other qualities discomforts them. They discover here the admission of and even the apology for that secret discrimination. The anti-Semitic types mentioned above can shift by certain mechanisms into different brands of Jew-lovers and overcompensate their hatred by a somewhat exaggerated and therefore fundamentally unreliable adoration. For instance, corresponding to the "born" anti-Semite is the man who always speaks of his enjoyable experiences with the Jewish people; to the anti-Semitic sectarian, all the Christian religious sects which venerate the Jews as the people of the Bible, keep the Sabbath, etc.; to the socialite anti-Semite, the well-bred gentleman who finds rowdy anti-Semitism repulsive.

Section V The Jews in society

It is necessary to seek an explanation of the causes of certain Jewish character traits to which the anti-Semite reacts negatively. These causes find their roots in the economic life of the Jew, in his particular function in society and in the consequences of his economic activity.

(a) The "dirty work"

The economic activity of the Jews is largely restricted to commerce and finance because of their exclusion from the immediately productive occupations. With the increasing significance of the market in capitalist economy, the importance of trade and finance increases too. A market economy accentuates the differences among the various strata of society. The lower strata become aware of their miserable conditions not so much through intercourse with those who are really mighty (the leaders of industry and politics) but through contact with the middleman, the merchant and banker. Their hatred of these middlemen explodes in the direction of the Jews who symbolize this element.

From olden times the practice of extending credit has prevented the antagonism between the possessors of power and the economically oppressed population from leading to recurrent catastrophes. The peasant and burgher, heavily burdened by taxes, could keep their heads above water for a long time by the utilization of credit. Yet the real economic situation about which they are deceived by the institution of credit does not improve, but becomes worse; one day the bill will be presented. And the middleman, largely the Jew, who has fulfilled a function indispensable to the existence of that society, appears as the casual factor of impoverishment. The outdated theories of Sombart about the role of the Jews in modern economy will be criticized in the course of this presentation.

(b) Non-productive capital

The diffusion of slogans about the difference between productive and non-productive capital originates as a manoeuver of distraction. This thesis, quite old in itself, was propagated during the struggle between the individual industrial groups and banking capital, between export industry and heavy industry, and between general directors and shareholders. During the period of inflation and deflation, the big German concerns deposited the burdens of the World War upon the shoulders of the middle and lower classes and renewed their productive equipment. They used the bankers and the Jews, together with the originators of the Versailles Treaty, as scapegoats for the misery of the post-war period. The figure of the so-called productive man was contrasted with that of the parasite. The experiences of the masses with the middleman serve to facilitate the resurrection and acceptance of the myth of the Jew as a non-productive parasite. It is difficult for the consumer to understand the economic necessity of the intermediary functions (commerce, advertising, achievements of financial technique) which serve to raise the price of a product; it is easier for him to understand the immediate functions of the production of goods. Hence, so many of the Utopian schemes of the last few centuries proposed a society in which the intermediary functions would be completely eliminated. Such a proposal, for example, appears in Richard Wagner's imaginary world. He contrasts the heroic productive Siegfried, a mixture of the munition manufacturer, the condottiere, and the rowdy, with the dwarf, a symbol of the owners, merchants, and the resentful, eternally complaining proletariat. The anti-Semitic declaration that one part of society consists of parasites feeding upon the other social strata cannot be overcome simply by being labeled a frame-up. Its historical origin must be clarified and understood.

(c) Rational law

Since its Roman origin, civil law has been the law of creditors. Whereas it recognizes no difference between any groups or individuals but aims at the universal protection of property, it is *a priori* antagonistic to the debtor. Historically, because of the creditor role of the Jews, deriving from their functions as bankers and merchants, we find them usually on the side of rational law. Their foes, on the other hand, favor a vague natural law based on the "sound instinct of the people."

There is real justification for the indignation of the condemned and foreclosed peasant or the widow plunged into poverty by law. They feel that an injustice has been done them because they have fallen into misery without any moral guilt on their part. The law, however, acts only as the executor of economic tendencies within the totality of society, and these condemn certain social strata to annihilation. As an abstract category, the law is not only innocent but to a considerable degree often acts as a check upon those tendencies. The conscientious man, deprived of his property by judicial verdicts, struggling in vain against his Jewish adversary and his Jewish lawyer, is a standing figure (for example in literature, e.g., *The Merchant of Venice* and many modern works).

(d) The Jewish mentality

The psychological faculty of abstraction developed with the commercial and financial function. In the commodity economy, men face each other as equals, not according to distinctions of birth or religion. It does not matter who they are, but only what commodity they want to buy or sell. The abstract notion of the thing as a commodity corresponds to the abstract notion of man. It makes no difference if one sells art objects, cotton or guns. The psychological functions which are developed on the basis of such economic conditions and the mentality which corresponds to them are of course not limited to the Jews. Calculating, so-called rationalistic thinking, has been developed chiefly by non-Jewish philosophers. Anti-Semitism, however, seeks to identify the Jews with this school of thought. As a matter of fact, the Jews historically have always had an affinity for dauntless, abstract thinking which manifests itself in the idea of a god who regards all men as equal. But this is not the whole story. There is also a "night side" to the Jewish spirit, full of irrationality and even mythology (one thinks of Jewish mystical sects such a Chassidism and of the Jewish superstition that still survives). In any event, even if one assumes that "rationalism" is the main trend among Jews, one has no reason whatsoever to bow to the verdict which anti-Semites reach on the basis of that assumption. The leveling that results from abstract thinking is a prerequisite for the development of the world, in a truly human sense, for this type of thinking divests human relationships and things of their taboos and brings them into the realm of reason. Jews have therefore always stood in the front ranks of the struggle for democracy and freedom.

The study of the so-called Jewish mentality explains why the Jews are blamed simultaneously for capitalistic and revolutionary, relativistic and dogmatic, tolerant and intolerant "mindedness." Such contradictory accusations do not in fact reflect upon the Jews but rather upon the state of mankind in the present historical period. The Jews are but the bearers of society's inconsistencies.

(e) The so-called race factor

The question of the origin of those qualities which, in distorted form, are attributed to the Jews, must be answered first by refuting the race theory.

As shown in the previous subsections, they are not biological but historical phenomena, characterized chiefly by the economic function into which the Jews have been forced. This explanation must not be applied automatically, however, for we see that certain intellectual and character traits are found, in a differentiated form, among Jewish individuals and families who have not themselves engaged in the occupations with which "Jewish" traits were originally connected. It is just this fact which is cited again and again by race theorists as proof of an alleged biological heritage.

The results of modern psychology may be applied to this social problem with good prospects of success. We follow the trend of modern psychology so far as to accept the thesis that just those decisive character traits which prove to be relatively constant in the individual's life may be traced back to the history and experiences of the child in his first years. In his earliest period of life, the child does not come into direct contact with the contemporary social milieu but only with his nearest of kin. Even they communicate with him less in accordance with their rational convictions than with behaviors (drive tendencies and impulses) which had been instilled in them during the earliest stages of their own lives. But it can be shown that the greatest impression on the infant is made not by the meaning of the words but by the expression, the voice, the movements of the parents. The soul of learning is imitation. The child's faculty of imitating the expressions of adults is exceedingly subtle. He observes the most unnoticeable and subtle shades of their gestures. Thus it happens that inclinations, skills, anxieties which have long lost their real meaning leave their mark on the faces and the behavior of later generations.

The development of this theory in detail can contribute not merely to a refutation of the race theory but to a positive replacement of it. It will throw light on the genesis of German, French, and English character traits as well as of Jewish traits. Even anti-Semitism itself will become more comprehensible in that the seemingly natural aversion to certain behaviors, for instance what might be called the home-grown anti-Semitism of some parts of Germany before National Socialism, may be explained as a psychological transmission from earlier historical conditions.

Section VI Foundations of National Socialist anti-Semitism

An understanding of anti-Jewish measures under National Socialism presupposes an understanding of the Nazi social and political system.

(a) Antecedent history of National Socialism

The roots of National Socialism in German and in European history in general have already been discussed in sections II and III. A survey of German philosophy and literature from the beginning of the twentieth century will show that most ideological features, such as anti-rationalism, community-madness, and the belief in a leader, have for some time dominated public thinking. We shall analyze the political pre-history of National Socialism, the Jingoism of the pre-war period to which, in spite of its anti-Semitic features, many Jews fell victim; we shall also seek to understand the specific characteristics on the basis of which the German people were aroused in 1914 and in the consequent war policy as features of the same historical roots from which National Socialism has developed. The political reasons for the decay of the Weimar Republic can be grouped into two categories: (1) The impossibility of a working parliament because of the dispossession of the middle classes. (The Communists, Social Democrats, and National Socialists together held 55.9 per cent of all the votes in December 1930.) The democratic parties therefore accepted the undemocratic practice of allowing the executive to rule by emergency decrees without the sanction of parliament, or at least of its committees. (2) The policy of toleration and alliance between the German democratic powers and the Prussian Junkers and the politically most backward sections of German heavy industry. The fact that the Junkers and heavy industry finally abandoned collaboration with the democrats and agreed to the seizure of power by the National Socialists cannot be explained primarily by their love for the new system. To face the dilemma of national as well as international danger, the help of the democratic forces was not strong enough. They chose dictatorship with no clear idea of what was to come. In the Weimar Republic the democratic powers were very weak from the beginning. As between the two extremes of the old ruling class and the radical sector of the workers, they decided in favor of the former without first being able to build up a strong policy of their own. (The project will carefully trace the individual stages of this process; alliances between the trade unions and Stinnes, between Ebert and Hindenburg, between the government and the fascist free corps, acceptance of the rearmament policy, and so forth. The terrorism of today's concentration camps was anticipated in the murder of republican leaders (Erzberger, Rathenau, Haase).) The surrender of the executive powers to the Junker loving Hindenburg, with the consent of all the democratic parties, sealed the fate of the Republic.

(b) The change in the function of money

In a laissez-faire economy the entrepreneur could tell by the increase or decrease of the money capital which he invested in an undertaking, the extent to which it was useful to society. If a factory or any other business could not keep pace with general economic developments, this was expressed in its financial statements and finally in the disappearance of the undertaking itself. Its collapse was the judgment of the market as to its social usefulness, and this judgment was proclaimed in money. In the totalitarian state the free market is abolished, and the ability of money to "declare" ceases to exist. Now the government, together with rather small groups of the contemporary German bureaucracy, determines which undertakings are useful for its military and other purposes and which are not. The market, an anonymous and democratic tribunal, is replaced by the command and plan of those in power.

The importance of the initiative of private entrepreneurs, particularly of large and small private banks, disappears. Bankers in non-totalitarian countries sometimes reveal a sympathy for National Socialism but they have an incomplete understanding of its economic character. At this point certain figures may be mentioned: Total deposits in German private banks between 1929 and 1938 have decreased from 2,300,000,000 to 950,000,000 marks, and in all the large banking concerns, from 12,408,000,000 to 6,804,000,000. Restriction of new issues of bonds, shares, and mortgage bonds has reduced operations on the stock market to a minimum. State-directed foreign exchange control and the compulsion to sell foreign exchange, bonds, and shares to the Reichsbank further reduce banking activity. The amount of Reich loans to be subscribed by the banks is determined, to a large extent, by the Reich itself. Credit as a whole is replaced by government protection. What applies to the banks applies in part to commerce as well.

The decline in importance of the spheres of economic activity in which the German Jews were chiefly engaged is the basis of their becoming superfluous. Their economic existence was intimately connected with the liberal system of economy and with its judicial and political conditions. In liberalism, as already mentioned, the unfit are eliminated by the effectiveness of the mechanism of competition, no matter what their names are or what personal qualities they have. In the totalitarian system, however, individuals or entire social groups can be sent to the gallows at any moment for political or other reasons. The replacement of the market by a planned economy of the state bureaucracy and the decline of the power of money capital makes possible the policy against the Jews in the Third Reich.

(c) *The propaganda value of anti-Semitism*

The above conditions alone, however, are not sufficient to explain the maintenance and intensification of anti-Semitic measures. The weight of the fortunes stolen from the Jews for the totalitarian economy is only one of the factors operative, although quite a strong one. But what is the effect of anti-Semitic propaganda upon certain social strata of other countries? While frank disgust for the anti-Semitism of the government is revealed among the German masses, the promises of anti-Semitism are eagerly swallowed where fascist governments have never been attempted. Even where the anti-Semitic sympathies of the masses are not yet tolerated, or even not yet conscious to them because of a cultural democratic tradition, the social and psychological tendencies which veer in that direction are effective and can become activized from one day to the next. The German government is highly sensitive to these circumstances. Behind the pro-Semitic speeches of the educated it scents an opportunity for psychological guidance of the people toward anti-Semitic aims. It is a master in linking its policies to existing or potential tensions in foreign countries. As religion formerly won foreign soil for civilization and for home industry, today the missionaries of anti-Semitism conquer the world for barbarism and German exports.

Section VII Experimental section

In this section the project plans to make the novel, and in the opinion of its directors, promising attempt to treat the phenomenon of anti-Semitism experimentally. This investigation will provide a series of experimental situations which approximate as closely as possible the concrete conditions of present day life. Its aim will be to visualize the mechanism of anti-Semitic reactions realistically. In this way it is hoped to develop the typology drafted in section IV. At the same time, an attempt will be made to direct the experiments in such a way as to provide insights into differences of regional and social groupings in regard to anti-Semitism.

The most satisfactory method of experimentation appears to be the use of certain films to be presented to subjects of different regional and social groups. Reactions of the subjects will be obtained partly by observation of their behavior during the performances, partly by interviews, partly by their written reports of their impressions. Naturally, the element of introspection cannot be entirely eliminated, but by careful and critical interpretation of results it is hoped to reduce the flaws to a minimum.

The following example may give an idea of the plan: A film will be made, showing boys of twelve to fifteen at play. An argument and a fight ensue. The relation of guilt and innocence is difficult to untangle. The scene ends, however, with one boy being thrashed by the others. Two versions of the film will be made. In one, the thrashed boy will be played by a Gentile, in the other by a Jew. Another variation will be introduced by showing each of these versions with two different dramatis personæ. In one version, the thrashed boy will bear a Jewish name, and in the other a Christian name.

Thus the film will be shown in four different combinations:

1) The thrashed boy is a Gentile with a Gentile name.
2) The thrashed boy is a Gentile with a Jewish name.
3) The thrashed boy is a Jew with a Gentile name.
4) The thrashed boy is a Jew with a Jewish name.

In any one case each of these combinations will be shown to only one group of subjects, for instance, to high-school boys or unemployed groups, who will not be informed in advance of the aim of the experiment. After the show, they will be told that the problem is the psychology of witness testimony. They will be cross-examined about what occurred, the question of guilt, the brave or cowardly behavior of the thrashed boy, etc. By comparing the testimony of the groups which have seen one version of the film with that of the groups which have seen the other version, it will be possible to reach conclusions about the extent of discrimination between Jews and Gentiles in perception and judgment.

Further variations are of course possible. For instance, all four versions may be presented to the same group in succession after longer intervals. The results of questioning immediately after the performance of the film will be supplemented by shorthand notes of remarks made by the audience during the performance. These notes will be taken by a person who will be present in the room but separated from the audience by a thin wall. If, for instance, it becomes evident that during the performance the thrashed boy with a Jewish name is defended by some of the participants and attacked by others, whereas at the end the witnesses reveal a united anti-Semitic influence, a contribution to the problem of susceptibility to anti-Semitic influence will have been made. The possibilities of variation are much richer than can be indicated here. It is planned to present the film not only in different social milieus in cities of the state of New York but also in other states. We hope to secure the collaboration of local universities and institutes for this purpose. The value of the results will depend to a large degree upon the number of experimental series undertaken in every milieu.

We believe that through this and similar experiments, a way will be found to study the distribution of anti-Semitism in the United States. Even though these methods have their margin of error, we believe that others have larger ones. When asked by questionnaires or interviewers, people will often reply, in accordance with their conscious conviction of the equality of human rights, that they have nothing against the Jews. In the experiment, however, where the question of anti-Semitism is not directly raised, the secret drives will appear clearly in the unconscious influencing of judgment. If extensive experimental series are undertaken in the various social milieus and in different parts of America, a rather objective picture of the anti-Semitic problem in this country may be gained. It will be especially interesting to reach those regions where few Jews live and where German propaganda works unfettered, for instance, in some states of the Northwest.

NOTES

The editor's notes, or editorial additions to Adorno's notes, are enclosed in square brackets.

1 Cf. Lee J. Levinger, *The Causes of Anti Semitism in the United States.* Philadelphia, 1925, p. 102 ff. [Adorno cites Levinger's thesis, later published as *Anti-Semitism in the United States; its History and Causes.* New York: Bloch, 1925. Reprinted Westport, Conn.: Greenwood Press, 1972.]

2 For example, Simmel's discourse on the stranger in his *Sociology*, Leipzig, 1908. [G. Simmel, 'The Stranger.' In K. Wolff (ed.), *The Sociology of Georg Simmel.* Glencoe: Free Press, 1950.]

3 Cf. "Von den Juden und ihren Lugen," *Ausgewählte Werke*, Ergänzungsreihe dritter Band, München 1936, pp. 94–5. [translated as *The Jews and their Lies*, Los Angeles: Christian Nationalist Crusade, 1948. The provenance of the translation underlines Adorno's point.]

4 Ibid., p. 63.

5 Ibid., p. 187.

6 Ibid., p. 191.

7 Ibid., p. 193.

8 Ibid., p. 189.

9 Ibid., p. 190.

10 Ibid., p. 191.

11 [*Essai sur les moeurs et l'esprit des nations* (two volumes). Paris: Garnier, 1963. Translated by T. Nugent as *An Essay on Universal History and the Manners and Spirit of Nations.* London, 1759.]

12 15 December 1773, letter to Chevalier de Lisle. [In *Complete Works*, Volume 124. Banbury: Voltaire Foundation, 1975.]

13 [*Sämtliche Werke*, Band XXIV. Hildesheim: Georg Olms, 1968, pp. 61–75.]

14 Kant, *Anthropology*, Part k, B § 46, footnote. [*Anthropology from a Pragmatic Point of View*, trans. and ed. M.J. Gregor. Hague: Nijhoff, 1974.]

15 Fichte, *About the French Revolution*, Book I, Chapter III, pp. 114 and 115. ['*Beitrag zur Berichtung der Urtheile des Publikums über die französische Revolution,*' in *Gesamtausgabe* Band 1.1. Stuttgart: Friedrich Frommann Verlag, 1964.]

16 Hegel, *Fragments of Theological Studies,* published by Karl Rosenkranz, in *G.W.F. Hegel's Life*, Berlin 1844, pp. 492, 522. [G.W.F. Hegel, *On Christianity: Early Theological Writings* (ed. R. Kroner). New York: Harper, p. 204ff.]

17 Hegel, *Phenomenology of Mind*, II, p. 257. [G.W.F. Hegel, *Phenomenology of Mind* (trans. A.V. Miller and ed. J. Findlay). Oxford: Oxford University Press, 1977, p. 206.]

18 E.g., Goethe, *Wilhelm Meister's Lehrjahre* (Book II, Chapters VI and XI). [*Wilhelm Meister's Years of Apprenticeship*, trans. H.M. Waidson. London: Calder, 1978.]

19 Goethe, *Faust*, verse 2839, 1842; trans. Anna Swanwick, London, 1886. [There are a number of other translations, for example *Goethe's Faust*, trans. B. Fairley. Toronto: University of Toronto Press, 1970.]

20 ['*Briefe aus der Schweiz,*' in *Sämtliche Werke*, Band 2.2. Carl Hauser Verlag: Munich.]

21 [H. von Treitschke, *History of Germany in the Nineteenth Century* (ed. and abridged G.A. Craig). Chicago: University of Chicago Press, 1975, p. 104.]

4

ANTI-SEMITISM AND FASCIST PROPAGANDA

The observations contained in this paper are based upon three studies made by the Research Project on Anti-Semitism[1] under the auspices of the Institute of Social Research at Columbia University. These studies analyze an extensive body of anti-democratic and anti-Semitic propaganda, consisting mainly of shorthand transcriptions of radio addresses by some West Coast agitators, pamphlets, and weekly publications. They are primarily of a psychological nature, although they often touch upon economic, political and sociological problems. Consequently, it is the psychological aspect of propaganda analysis rather than the objective content of this propaganda which is here under consideration. Neither a comprehensive treatment of the methods employed, nor an enunciation of a full-fledged psychoanalytic theory of anti-democratic propaganda has been aimed at. Further, facts and interpretations, generally known to those familiar with psychoanalysis have been omitted. The goal has been, rather, to point out some findings, which, however preliminary and fragmentary, may suggest further psychoanalytic evaluation.

The material studied itself evinces a psychological approach. It is conceived in psychological rather than in objective terms. It aims at winning people over by *playing upon their unconscious mechanisms* rather than by presenting ideas and arguments. Not only is the oratorical technique of the fascist demagogues of a shrewdly illogical, pseudo-emotional nature; more than that, positive political programs, postulates, nay any concrete political ideas play but a minor role compared with the psychological stimuli applied to the audience. It is from these stimuli and from other information rather than from the vague, confused platforms of the speeches that we can identify them as fascist at all.

Let us consider three characteristics of the predominantly psychological approach of current American fascist propaganda.

(1) It is *personalized* propaganda, essentially non-objective. The

162

agitators spend a large part of their time in speaking either about themselves or about their audiences. They present themselves as lone wolves, as healthy, sound American citizens with robust instincts, as unselfish and indefatigable; and they incessantly divulge real or fictitious intimacies about their lives and those of their families. Moreover, they appear to take a warm human interest in the small daily worries of their listeners, whom they depict as poor but honest, common-sense but non-intellectual, native Christians. They identify themselves with their listeners and lay particular emphasis upon being simultaneously both modest little men and leaders of great calibre. They often refer to themselves as mere messengers of him who is to come – a trick already familiar in Hitler's speeches. This technique is probably closely related to the substitution of a collective ego for paternal imagery.[2] Another favorite scheme of personalization is to dwell upon petty financial needs and to beg for small amounts of money. The agitators disavow any pretense to superiority, implying that the leader to come is one who is as weak as his brethren but who dares to confess his weakness without inhibition, and is consequently going to be transformed into the strong man.

(2) All these demagogues substitute means for ends. They prate about "this great movement," about their organization, about a general American revival they hope to bring about, but they very rarely say anything about what such a movement is supposed to lead to, what the organization is good for or what the mysterious revival is intended positively to achieve. Here is a typical example of a redundant description of the revival idea by one of the most successful West Coast agitators:

My friend, there is not but one way to get a revival and all America has got to get that revival, all of the churches. The story of the great Welsh revival is simply this. Men become desperate for the holiness of God in the world, and they began to pray, and they began to ask to send a revival(!) and wherever men and women went the revival was on.

The glorification of action, of something going on, simultaneously obliterates and replaces the purpose of the so-called movement. The end is "that we might demonstrate to the world that there are patriots, God-fearing Christian men and women who are yet willing to give their lives to the cause of God, home and native land.[3]"

(3) Since the entire weight of this propaganda is to promote the means, propaganda itself becomes the ultimate content. In other words,

propaganda functions as a kind of *wish-fulfillment*. This is one of its most important patterns. People are "let in," they are supposedly getting the inside dope, taken into confidence, treated as of the elite who deserve to know the lurid mysteries hidden from outsiders. Lust for snooping is both encouraged and satisfied. Scandal stories, mostly fictitious, particularly of sexual excesses and atrocities are constantly told; the indignation at filth and cruelty is but a very thin, purposely transparent rationalization of the pleasure these stories convey to the listener. Occasionally a slip of the tongue occurs by which scandal mongering can easily be identified as an end in itself. Thus a certain West Coast demagogue once promised to give in his next speech full details about a phony decree of the Soviet Government organizing the prostitution of Russian womanhood. In announcing this story, the speaker said that there was not a real he-man whose backbone would not tingle upon hearing these facts. The ambivalence implied in this "tingling backbone" device is evident.

To a certain extent, all these patterns can be explained rationally. Very few American agitators would dare openly to profess fascist and anti-democratic goals. In contrast to Germany, the democratic ideology in this country has evolved certain taboos, the violation of which might jeopardize people engaging in subversive activities. Thus the fascist demagogue here is much more restricted in what he can say, for reasons of both political censorship and psychological tactics. Moreover, a certain vagueness with regard to political aims is inherent in Fascism itself. This is partly due to its intrinsically untheoretical nature, partly to the fact that its followers will be cheated in the end and that therefore the leaders must avoid any formulation to which they might have to stick later. It should also be noted that with regard to terror and repressive measures, Fascism habitually goes *beyond* what it has announced. Totalitarianism means knowing no limits, not allowing for any breathing spell, conquest with absolute domination, complete extermination of the chosen foe. With regard to this meaning of fascist "dynamism," any clear-cut program would function as a limitation, a kind of guarantee even to the adversary. It is essential to totalitarian rule that nothing shall be guaranteed, no limit is set to ruthless arbitrariness.

Finally we should bear in mind that totalitarianism regards the masses not as self-determining human beings who rationally decide their own fate and are therefore to be addressed as rational subjects, but that it treats them as mere objects of administrative measures who are taught, above all, to be self-effacing and to obey orders.

However, just this last point requires a somewhat closer scrutiny if it is to mean more than the hackneyed phrase about mass hypnosis under

Fascism. It is highly doubtful whether actual mass hypnosis takes place at all in Fascism, or whether it is not a handy metaphor that permits the observer to dispense with further analysis. Cynical soberness is probably more characteristic of the fascist mentality than psychological intoxication. Moreover, no one who has ever had an opportunity to observe fascist attitudes can overlook the fact that even those stages of collective enthusiasm to which the term "mass hypnosis" refers have an element of conscious manipulation, by the leader and even by the individual subject himself, which can hardly be regarded as a result of mere passive contagion. Speaking psychologically, the ego plays much too large a role in fascist irrationality to admit of an interpretation of the supposed ecstasy as a mere manifestation of the unconscious. There is always something self-styled, self-ordained, spurious about fascist hysteria which demands critical attention if the psychological theory about Fascism is not to yield to the irrational slogans which Fascism itself promotes.

What, now, does the fascist, and in particular, the anti-Semitic propaganda speech wish to achieve? To be sure, its goal is not "rational," for it makes no attempt to convince people, and it always remains on a non-argumentative level. In this connection two facts deserve detailed investigation:

(1) Fascist propaganda attacks bogies rather than real opponents, that is to say, it builds up an *imagery* of the Jew, or of the Communist, and tears it to pieces, without caring much how this imagery is related to reality.

(2) It does not employ discursive logic but is rather, particularly in oratorical exhibitions, what might be called an organized flight of ideas. The relation between premises and inferences is replaced by a linking-up of ideas resting on mere similarity, often through association by employing the same characteristic word in two propositions which are logically quite unrelated. This method not only evades the control mechanisms of rational examination, but also makes it psychologically easier for the listener to "follow." He has no exacting thinking to do, but can give himself up passively to a stream of words in which he swims.

In spite of these patterns of retrogression, however, anti-Semitic propaganda is by no means altogether irrational. The term, irrationality, is much too vague to describe sufficiently so complex a psychological phenomenon. We know, above all, that fascist propaganda, with all its twisted logic and fantastic distortions, is consciously planned and organized. If it is to be called irrational, then it is applied rather than spontaneous irrationality, a kind of psychotechnics reminiscent of the calculated effect conspicuous in most presentations of today's mass culture – such as in movies and broadcasts. Even if it is true, however, that the mentality of the fascist agitator resembles somewhat the muddle-headedness of his prospective followers, and that the leaders themselves "are hysterical or even paranoid types," they have learned, from vast experience and from the striking example of Hitler, how to utilize their own neurotic or psychotic dispositions for ends which are wholly adapted to the principle of reality (*realitaetsgerecht*). Conditions prevailing in our society tend to transform neurosis and even mild lunacy into a commodity which the afflicted can easily sell, once he has discovered that many others have an affinity for his own illness. The fascist agitator is usually a masterly salesman of his own psychological defects. This is possible only because of a general structural similarity between followers and leader, and the goal of propaganda is to establish a concord between them rather than to convey to the audience any ideas or emotions which were not their own from the very beginning. Hence, the problem of the true psychological nature of fascist propaganda may be formulated: Of what does this rapport between leader and followers in the propaganda situation consist?

A first lead is offered by our observation that this type of propaganda functions as a gratification. We may compare it with the social phenomenon of the soap opera. Just as the housewife, who has enjoyed the sufferings and the good deeds of her favorite heroine for a quarter of an hour over the air, feels impelled to buy the soap sold by the sponsor, so the listener to the fascist propaganda act, after getting pleasure from it, accepts the ideology represented by the speaker out of gratitude for the show. "Show" is indeed the right word. The achievement of the self-styled leader is a performance reminiscent of the theater, of sport, and of so-called religious revivals. It is characteristic of the fascist demagogues that they boast of having been athletic heroes in their youth. This is how they behave. They shout and cry, fight the Devil in pantomime, and take off their jackets when attacking "those sinister powers."

The fascist leader types are frequently called hysterical. No matter how their attitude is arrived at, their hysterical behavior fulfills a certain function. Though they actually resemble their listeners in most respects, they differ from them in an important one: they know no inhibitions in expressing themselves. They function vicariously for their inarticulate listeners by doing and saying what the latter would like to, but either cannot or dare not. They violate the taboos which middle-class society has put upon any expressive behavior on the part of the normal, matter-of-fact citizen. One may say that some of the effect of fascist propaganda is achieved by this break-through. The fascist agitators are taken seriously because they risk making fools of themselves.

Educated people in general found it hard to understand the effect of Hitler's speeches because they sounded so insincere, ungenuine, or, as the German word goes, *verlogen.* But it is a deceptive idea, that the so-called common people have all unfailing flair for the genuine and sincere, and disparage fake. Hitler was liked, not in spite of his cheap antics, but just because of them, because of his false tones and his clowning. They are observed as such, and appreciated. Real folk artists, such as Girardi[4] with his *Fiakerlied,* were truly in touch with their audiences and they always employed what strikes us as "false tones." We find similar manifestations regularly in drunkards who have lost their inhibitions. The sentimentality of the common people is by no means primitive, unreflecting emotion. On the contrary, it is pretense, a fictitious, shabby imitation of real feeling, often self-conscious and slightly contemptuous of itself. This fictitiousness is the life element of the fascist propagandist performances.

The situation created by this exhibition may be called a *ritual* one. The fictitiousness of the propagandist oratory, the gap between the speaker's personality and the content and character of his utterances are ascribable to the ceremonial role assumed by and expected of him. This ceremony, however, is merely a symbolic revelation of the identity that he verbalizes, an identity the listeners feel and think, but cannot express. This is what they actually want him to do, neither being convinced nor, essentially, being whipped into a frenzy, but having their own minds expressed to them. The gratification they get out of propaganda consists most likely in the demonstration of this identity, no matter how far it actually goes, for it is a kind of institutionalized redemption of their own inarticulateness through the speaker's verbosity. This act of revelation, and the temporary abandonment of responsible, self-contained serious-ness is the decisive pattern of the propagandist ritual. To be sure, we may call this act of identification a phenomenon of collective retrogression. It is not simply a reversion to older, primitive emotions but rather the reversion toward a ritualistic attitude in which the expression of emotions is sanctioned by an agency of social control. In this context it is interesting to note that one of the most successful and dangerous West Coast agitators again and again encouraged his listeners to indulge in all sorts of emotions, to give way to their feelings, to shout and to shed tears, persist-ently attacking the behavior pattern of rigid self-control brought about by the established religious denominations and by the whole Puritan tradition.

This loosening of self-control, the merging of one's impulses with a ritual scheme is closely related to the universal psychological weakening of the self-contained individual.

A comprehensive theory of fascist propaganda would be tantamount to a psychoanalytic deciphering of the more or less rigid ritual performed in each and every fascist address. The scope of this paper permits only brief reference to some characteristics of this ritual.

(1) There is, above all, the amazing stereotypy of all the fascist propaganda material known to us. Not only does each individual speaker incessantly repeat the same patterns again and again, but different speakers use the same clichés. Most important, of course, is the dichotomy of black and white, foe and friend. Stereotypy applies not only to the defamation of the Jews or to political ideas, such as the denunciation of Communism or of banking capital, but also to apparently very remote matters and attitudes. We have summarized a list of typical psychological devices employed by practically all fascist agitators, which could be boiled down to no more than thirty formulas.[5] Many of them have already been mentioned, such as the lone wolf device, the idea of indefatigability, of persecuted innocence, of the great little man, the praise of the movement as such, and so forth. Of course, the uniformity of these devices can in part be accounted for by reference to common source, such as Hitler's *Mein Kampf*, or even by an organizational linking of all the agitators, as was apparently the case on the West Coast. But the reason must be sought elsewhere if the agitators in many different parts of the country employ the same specific assertions, e.g. their lives have been threatened and their listeners will know who is responsible if the threat is carried out – an incident that never occurs. These patterns are standardized for psychological reasons. The prospective fascist follower craves this rigid repetition, just as the jitterbug craves the standard pattern of popular songs and gets furious if the rules of the game are not strictly observed. Mechanical application of these patterns is one of the essentials of the ritual.

(2) It is not accidental that many persons with a fake religious attitude are found among the fascist agitators. This, of course, has a sociological aspect which will be discussed later. Psychologically, however, the carry-overs of by-gone religion, neutralized and void of any specific dogmatic content, are put to the service of the fascist ritualistic attitude. Religious language and religious forms are utilized in order to lend the impression of a sanctioned ritual that is performed again and again by some "community."

(3) The specific religious content as well as the political one is replaced by something which may briefly be designated the *cult of the existent*. The attitude which Else Brunswik has called "identification with a *status quo*" is closely related to this cult. The devices pointed out in McClung Lee's

book on Father Coughlin,[6] such as the band wagon idea or the testimony trick, implying the support of famous or successful people, are only elements of a much farther-reaching pattern of behavior. It signifies explicitly that whatever *is*, and thus has established its strength, is also right, – the sound principle to be followed. One of the West Coast agitators occasionally even directed his listeners generally to follow the advice of their leaders without specifying what kind of leaders he meant. Leadership as such, devoid of any visible idea or aim is glorified. Making a fetish of reality and of established power relationships is what tends, more than anything else, to induce the individual to give himself up and to join the supposed wave of the future.

(4) One of the intrinsic characteristics of the fascist ritual is *innuendo*, sometimes followed by the actual revelation of the facts hinted at, but more often not. Again a rational reason for this trend can easily be given: either the law or at least prevailing conventions preclude open statements of a pro–Nazi or anti–Semitic character, and the orator who wants to convey such ideas has to resort to more indirect methods. It seems likely, however, that innuendo is employed, and enjoyed, as a gratification *per se*. For example, the agitator says "those dark forces, you know whom I mean," and the audience at once understands that his remarks are directed against the Jews. The listeners are thus treated as an in-group who already know everything the orator wishes to tell them and who agree with him before any explanation is given. Concord of feeling and opinion between speaker and listener, which was mentioned before, is established by innuendo. It serves as a confirmation of the basic identity between leader and followers. Of course, the psychoanalytic implications of innuendo go far beyond these surface observations. Reference is made here to the role attributed by Freud to allusions in the interplay between the conscious and the unconscious. Fascist innuendo feeds upon this role.

(5) The performance of the ritual as such functions to a very large extent as the ultimate content of fascist propaganda. Psychoanalysis has shown the relatedness of ritual behavior to compulsion neurosis; and it is obvious that the typical fascist ritual of revelation is a substitute for sexual gratification. Beyond this, however, some speculation may be allowed with regard to the specific symbolic meaning of the fascist ritual. It is not wide off the mark to interpret it as the offering of a sacrifice. If the assumption is correct that the overwhelming majority of accusations and atrocity stories with which the fascist propaganda speeches abound, are projections of the wishes of the orators and their followers, the whole symbolic act of revelation celebrated in each propaganda speech expresses, however much concealed, the sacramental killing of the chosen

foe. At the hub of the fascist, anti-Semitic propaganda ritual is the desire for ritual murder. This can be corroborated by a piece of evidence from the everyday psychopathology of fascist propaganda. The important role played by the religious element in American fascist and anti-Semitic propaganda has been mentioned earlier. One of the Fascist West Coast radio priests said in a broadcast:

> Can you not see that unless we exalt the holiness of our God, that unless we proclaim the justice of God in this world of ours, unless we proclaim the fact of a heaven and of a hell, unless we proclaim the fact that without the remission, *without the shedding of blood*, there is no remission of sin? Cannot you see that only Christ and God are dominant and that revolution will ultimately take this nation of ours?

The transformation of Christian doctrine into slogans of political violence could not be cruder than in this passage. The idea of a sacrament, the "shedding of blood" of Christ, is straight-forwardly interpreted in terms of "shedding of blood" in general, with an eye to a political upheaval. The actual shedding of blood is advocated as necessary because the world has supposedly been redeemed by the shedding of Christ's blood. Murder is invested with the halo of a sacrament. Thus the ultimate reminder of the sacrificed Christ in fascist propaganda is *"Judenblut muss fliessen"* ("Jewish blood must be spilled"). Crucifixion is transformed into a symbol of the pogrom. Psychologically, all fascist propaganda is simply a system of such symbols.

At this point attention must be paid to destructiveness as the psychological basis of the fascist spirit. The programs are abstract and vague, the fulfillments are spurious and illusory because the promise expressed by fascist oratory is nothing but destruction itself. It is hardly accidental that all fascist agitators dwell upon the imminence of catastrophes of some kind. Whereas they warn of impending danger, they and their listeners get a thrill out of the idea of inevitable doom, without even making a clear-cut distinction between the destruction of their foes and of themselves. This mental behavior, by the way, could be clearly observed during the first years of Hitlerism in Germany, and has a deep archaic basis. One of the West Coast demagogues once said: "I want to say that you men and women, you and I are living in the most fearful time of the history of the world. We are living also in the most gracious and most wonderful time." This is the agitator's dream, a union of the horrible and the wonderful, a delirium of annihilation masked as salvation. The strongest hope for effectively countering this whole type of propaganda lies in pointing out its self-destructive implications. The unconscious psychological desire for self-annihilation faithfully reproduces the structure of a political movement which ultimately transforms its followers into victims.

NOTES

The editor's notes, or editorial additions to Adorno's notes, are enclosed in square brackets.

1   Authors: T.W. Adorno, Leo Lowenthal, Paul W. Massing. [Later published as follows. T.W. Adorno *et al.*, *The Authoritarian Personality*. New York: Harper & Row, 1950. L. Lowenthal and N. Guterman, *Prophets of Deceit: A Study of the Techniques of the American Agitator*. New York: Harper & Row, 1949. P. Massing, *Rehearsal for Destruction: A Study of Political Anti-Semitism in Imperial Germany*. New York: Harper & Row, 1949. Adorno does not refer to his own lengthy study of American fascist propaganda, written in around 1943, which elaborates the arguments of the present essay but which was not published in his lifetime: 'The Psychological Technique of Martin Luther Thomas's Radio Addresses.' *Gesammelte Schriften* 9.1. Frankfurt: Suhrkamp, 1975. The study is discussed in the 'Introduction' above.]

2   [Adorno inserted a note here: 'see pp. 8–9, this volume.' That is, M. Horkheimer, 'Sociological Background of the Psychoanalytic Approach,' in E. Simmel (ed.), *Anti-Semitism: A Social Disease*. New York: International Universities Press, 1946.]

3   All quotations are taken literally, without any change, from shorthand transcriptions. [The quotes are all from Martin Luther Thomas.]

4   Famous Viennese actor, around the turn of the century.

5   [Adorno analyzes thirty three 'devices' in 'The Psychological Technique of Martin Luther Thomas's Radio Addresses.']

6   [A. McClung Lee and E. Briant-Lee (eds), *The Fine Art of Propaganda: A Study of Father Coughlin's Speeches*. New York: Harcourt-Brace, 1939.]

NAME INDEX

Adorno, T.W.: assessment of 18, 23–8;
focus on anti-Semitism 22–3;
Freudianism 21–2; methodology
18–20; works:- "Anti-Semitism
and Fascist Propaganda" 1, 10;
The Authoritarian Personality 6–7,
20, 21, 23, 27, 121; "Elements of
Anti-Semitism" 4; *Minima Moralia*
1; "The Psychological Technique
of Martin Luther Thomas's Radio
Addresses" ("Thomas" study) 1,
10, 17, 19; "Research Project on
Anti-Semitism" 1, 3–6; "The Stars
Down to Earth" 1, 10, 17–18, 19,
24; Theses Against Occultism" 1, 15
Alger, H. 85
Allport, G. 21
Altemeyer, B. 21
Angus, I. 24
Arnold of Citeaux 139

Bakhtin, M. 24, 31 n.67
Baldwin, Archbishop of Canterbury
140
Balzac, H. de 147
Baudrillard, J. 28
Bauman, Z. 3, 23
Bebel, F.A. 138
Becket, Thomas à 140
Benjamin, W. 24
Berger, D. 29 n.9
Bergson, H. 78
Bernstein, J.M. 15, 25
Billig, M. 20, 22

Brecht, B. 16
Brickner, R.M. 35
Brittan, L. 4
Brunswik, E. 168

Comte, A. 116
Coughlin, Father 169

Denzin, N.K. 33 n.103
Derrida, J. 33 n.103
Descartes, R. 131
Devereux, G. 35

Ebert, F. 156
Endelman, T. 29 n.23
Erikson, E.H. 8, 105
Erzberger, M. 156

Fenichel, O. 12, 70
Fichte, J.G. 145, 146
Foucault, M. 33 n.103
Freud, S. 7, 8, 35, 43, 49, 60, 71, 169
Fromm, E. 55, 69–70

Girardi 167
Goebbels, J. 151
Goethe, J.W. von 4, 142, 146, 148
Gottschalk 139
Gramsci, A. 23

Haase, H. 156
Harris, D. 23
Hegel, G.W.F. 133, 134 n.6, 142,
145–6, 148

SUBJECT INDEX